MW00928882

The 18-Year Factor

How our upbringing affects our lives & relationships

by Steve Cornell

CONTENTS

RESTORING A BETTER FUTURE:
How can I rebuild for a healthy future?

Introduction

A medical doctor in his mid-fifties admitted, "About ten years ago, I finally came to terms with the negative effect my father had on me." His wife (also a doctor) was shaking her head affirmingly. He was unresolved for more than forty years and taking everyone else along for the ride.

Raw, afraid, and nervous

> Everything seemed even more unbearable because I could find no one to talk to...nowhere to unburden my troubled heart. I felt raw, afraid, and nervous to expose the painful things in my life. It seemed safer to keep on suppressing the memories.

After working through the pain of her troubled upbringing, this young lady (whose full story you'll read later) acknowledged, "It is good to look back at these things, to cease being pushed around, burdened by the past, to know that they are memories. I do not need to carry them around or relive them anymore."

Two people in one person

Another woman admitted living for many years with an unhealthy approval addiction. She recognized, "I did not want to disappoint others, so I created a false image of myself. I tried to look normal on the outside when everything within me was chaotic." You will meet her later as well.

Unresolved? Pushed around? Burdened? Carrying and reliving painful memories? Trying to look normal? Everything in me was chaotic? Many people identify with these experiences because they share in common the ongoing effects of a troubled upbringing. For more than 30 years, I've been privileged to help many people overcome the negative impacts.

According to Dr. Robert Block, the former President of the American Academy of Pediatrics, "Adverse childhood experiences are the single greatest unaddressed public health threat facing our nation today."[1]

The 18-Year Factor is a way of referring to the first 18 years of life—the most impressionable years. We all benefit from looking more closely at our upbringing—no matter what kind of home we experienced.

Our 18-year factor forms a kind of template for the way we *think*, how we *feel*, and how we *act*—especially in adult relationships. Through this book, I invite you to look back and understand how your upbringing affects your life and relationships.

Perhaps you ask, "What good will it do to look back?" "If we can't go back and change it, why bother thinking about it?" "Why get stuck in the past?" "Isn't it better to forget it and move on?" These questions (answered in chapter two) too often serve as deflective clichés for denying the ongoing effects of a painful past.

It's true that the only thing you can change about your past is how it affects you in your future. A better understanding of our history will help us *improve the way it affects our future*. View the messages in this book as an invitation to look more closely at the influences that shaped your life during your childhood years.

Key lines from *The 18-Year Factor*

- Attachments to a painful past make it difficult to do well in the present.
- The narrow lens of yesterday's loss doesn't have to control the way you see your future.
- Don't let the diagnosis define your destiny.
- Where you've been doesn't have to define who you become.
- Include the past in who you become instead of letting it define who you are.
- Overcoming a problem involves understanding *where* and *how* it originated.
- The only thing you can change about the past is how it affects the future.
- What you focus on is what will become your reality.
- The only person you can change is you. Get started!

Though the names have been changed, the captivating real-life stories throughout this book will help readers *think* more deeply and *talk* more openly about their own stories.

Stories in *The 18-Year Factor*

- A quiet domineering father.
- A dark secret that couldn't remain hidden.
- I carried my rock.
- How could I kill my father?
- An unhealthy approval addiction
- I hate my father so much.
- Where's that dummy son of mine?
- I go down to the basement.
- Hurt by a distant father.
- Your dad didn't want you.

- My father always told me I was stupid.
- The day my childhood ended.
- I get out of the car quickly.

Unexpected conversations

I've been fascinated by the way the title of this book has led to many unexpected conversations. The mere mention of *The 18-Year Factor: How Our Upbringing Affects Our Lives and Relationships* immediately prompted complete strangers to talk with me about deeply personal issues from their past.

During a writing retreat at a beautiful resort in Cape Cod, Massachusetts, I located what I thought was a quiet corner of a large foyer to write. I soon discovered, however, that my spot wasn't as private as I had thought. Throughout the week many people approached me to ask what I was doing. When I told them that I was writing a book, they all responded by asking what the book was about and I answered each person by stating the title. I consistently heard the same one-word response, always expressed with dismay. "Wow!"

Then the unexpected part came as most of them began to talk openly with me about their 18-year factor. Some of these people caught themselves midway into their story. "Wait! I think I've told you more about myself than I've ever told anyone and I don't even know you!" One man asked to sign his wife up for a counseling session with me. "I've been paying for years for what her father did to her!"

Is there a story behind your story?

Most people recall positive and negative experiences from their upbringing. If you had an overall healthy 18-year factor, you are part of a rapidly diminishing number of people. But even if you fall in that category, it doesn't mean you can't benefit from looking more closely at the influences that shaped the way you see yourself and relate to others.

For those who are married or planning to marry, this benefit is especially valid. Marriage is one of the primary contexts where 18-year-factor issues emerge. As many would attest, differences in upbringings are a familiar source of marital disagreements. We are wise to engage in more in-depth conversations about these differences before they become a source of conflict. I would argue that these conversations should be a required part of the preparation for marriage.

The way we communicate, resolve conflict, process anger and many other essential parts of life arise from our 18-year factor, the most impressionable years of our lives.

Dysfunctional homes are the new normal

American filmmaker Steven Spielberg struggled throughout adult life because of challenges tracing back to his 18-year factor. Although estrangement from his father was part of his story, his childhood years proved difficult for other reasons. As a young Jewish boy with awkward physical features (a big nose and ears that stuck out), coupled with living in a culture of anti-Semitism, Spielberg experienced constant ridicule and bullying. He acknowledged being "exquisitely uncomfortable" with himself.[2] After many years of struggle, (evident in the themes and characters of his movies), he advised a group of graduates, "Don't turn away from what's painful. Examine it. Challenge it."[3]

In a variety of ways, Spielberg's story of childhood pain and struggle is like the stories of many famous people. Years of struggle as an adult almost always trace back to a troubled 18-year factor.

Home is where the heart is (formed)

Exploring the 18-year factor takes us on a journey back to our childhood home. That journey affords us an opportunity to look closely at how the people, circumstances, and experiences of the past continue to affect our lives and relationships. The message of the well-known saying "Home is where the heart is" conjures up an image of an idyllic childhood home, but that is sadly not the way many people remember their upbringing. On the contrary, that saying is bad news for those who grew up in dysfunctional homes. Why? Because home is where the heart is *formed*.

The heart as treasure chest and control room

Unlike the literal heart, I'm using "heart" to refer to our inner person. Two images might help us understand what happens in the formation of our heart (inner person) during childhood years. First, think of a child's heart as a treasure chest in which parents and other experiences store things. These deposits in the treasure chest come in the form of messages about a child's identity and worth. Parents (or guardians) are the primary people who store things in a child's heart. The second image is of the heart as a control room for life. The mind (our way of thinking) contributes to the formation of the heart when we replay and reaffirm the messages deposited by others.

The normal process of growth from adolescence to adulthood (examined in more detail later) is a challenging journey of vulnerability regarding identity and security. When parents are unaware of the changes and challenges involved in this process of growth, they will likely contribute to it in ways that are either harmful or damaging. In the chapters ahead, we'll examine the vital role parents (and other adults) play in the formation of the inner person of a child. The messages they send either passively (by neglect) or actively (by abuse) stay with their children long into their adult lives.

From my years of experience as a counselor, I gained a deep passion for encouraging healthy relationships. To that end, I write this book in the hope that it will help many others in understanding, processing and resolving adverse effects from a painful past, with a distinctive focus on *integrating* the four dimensions of life to *restore the whole person*. I also hope it will help parents understand how to provide a healthy 18-year factor for their children.

Each chapter concludes with evaluation and discussion questions to encourage personal reflection and group discussion. A free printable set of the questions is available at www.the18yearfactor.com. Additionally, the appendices at the end of the book should aid in further evaluation.

EXPLORING THE PAST

Why look back into your past?

Chapter 1

Buckle up for a ride into the past

The idea that our past affects our present lives seems so simple and widely understood. Indeed, it's a major premise for the field of psychology. Surely everyone understands that the influences of parents, circumstances, and other experiences during childhood years carry on into adult life. Or, do they?

- **True or false?** Most people understand that their upbringing affects their lives. True.
- **True or false?** Most people understand how (and how much) their upbringing affects their lives. *False.*

Most adults who grew up in dysfunctional homes *know that* they had an unhealthy upbringing. However, most of these same people do not have a clear understanding of *how* (and *how much*) their past affects their present lives and relationships. As a result, they don't adequately recognize how unhealthy attachments to their past are hurting their relationships. Throughout this book, we will take a guided discovery of *how* and *how much* our opinions about life, ourselves, and our approach to relationships remain influenced by childhood years.

Those who weathered a painful past respond or react in different ways. We will explore these more fully throughout the book, but in the meantime, perhaps you might see your own reaction/response in one of these as you continue along the journey.

Four reactions to a painful past
1.   Ignoring the past
2.   Denying the past
3.   Accepting the past (in a self-defeated way)
4.   Perpetuating the past

Who benefits from looking back?

Evaluating the effects of your 18-year factor is helpful no matter your age or the kind of home in which you were raised. Through a guided approach, we gain a clearer understanding of the setting in which our identity was formed and why we instinctively act and react in certain ways as adults. Understanding *how* and *how much* a difficult upbringing affected us is essential for enjoying healthy relationships and for protecting those close to us from the adverse effects of a troubled past.

A word to those from "good homes"

I have a particular interest in speaking to those who came from healthy homes. Not only will this book benefit you, it will equip you to help those with a complicated and painful past. For those who want to overcome a dysfunctional upbringing, your role is vital. To that end, I will share valuable insights for counseling others.

Connecting past and present

The disruptive effects of a troubled upbringing typically become evident when they challenge adult relationships. Close relationships shine a light on suppressed experiences, causing them to surface in disruptive ways. For those who are married or who hope to be, take note: a guided look at the 18-year factor is particularly beneficial for YOU. Close and healthy relationships thrive on *vulnerability, transparency,* and *trust*—three difficult qualities for someone with a troubled past.

Going to the source

Rarely do attitudes, outlooks, and behaviors appear out of nowhere. There is almost always a history. Diane, a single woman who had been through a painful divorce, said to me, "Men change after they get married." I disagreed. I suggested that instead, men are hunters who camouflage until they "get their hunt." The camouflage then comes off and what you see is what you get. I gently remind her that sides to people don't appear without a history. Marriage problems are often single person problems brought into a marriage. Why didn't Diane see the man beneath the camouflage? Perhaps the blinding effects of the in-love experience keep people from looking too closely at a lover.

To understand another person and enjoy a healthy relationship, we must assess his or her 18-year factor. Exploring the effects of upbringing provides essential insights into a person's life. Our quality of life depends on how well we process the effects of our past.

Essential for marriage

For more than 25 years, I've taught a *Relationships 101* class. In this class, I remind singles that the relationship phase of dating tends to conceal information that a marriage relationship will later reveal. It's too often a fake-it-till-you-make-it time. I warn them that the euphoric delusional state of being in love blinds people to reality. Patiently exploring the 18-year factor will help to expose concealments and minimize surprises.

Special **word to men** (reluctant historians of a painful past)

Men are wired to be reluctant historians of their emotional past. They tend to mask pain behind a perceived obligation to "man up" in the face of hardships. "There's no time for licking your wounds or wallowing in the past," they believe—no sense in putting the past up for review because none of it can be changed. Those who travel in close company with these men tend to see things differently. They feel firsthand the lingering effects of their troubled past.

Male ego most often stands in the way, making men unwilling to consider the ongoing effects from past experiences. This stubborn pride comes with a price tag. Eventually, male ego loses strength when men enter their mid-forties. The defensive structure begins to deteriorate as youthful vision and energy dissipate and the melancholy of middle years settles in like a foggy day. This is the time, in my experience, when men start looking back and taking inventory. However, some at this time of life feel it's too late to benefit from a look back.

How could I kill my father? (Charlie's story)

Charlie, a seventy-year-old man who lived in an upscale retirement community, asked if he could talk with me. When we met, he told me his childhood story of repeatedly thinking about ways he could kill his father. He recalled lying in bed when he was only eight years old, listening to his father abuse his mother. This was a common part of family life. "All I could think about," he recalled, "was how I could kill my dad. I thought about using a kitchen knife or finding a gun, or hitting him really hard with some object." Charlie's home was a prison of fear and anger. He hated the man that should have been the most important person in his life. Home should be a safe place for children, a place filled with heartwarming memories. Charlie looked back on a place remembered for the fear and anger it produced.

How does it affect a young boy's emotional and psychological well-being when the most formative years of his life are lived in such an oppressive home? Should we expect him to struggle with identity issues? Do we expect it to influence his sense of security and affect his future relationships? He came to talk with me about his upbringing because his wife insisted that he see me. At seventy years old, he continued to battle feelings and fears connected with this part of his life that adversely affected his adult relationships.

Men will sometimes hold out on looking back until those who are close to them insist that they seek help for processing their past.

"I finally came to terms with the effect my father had on me" (Robert's story)

Robert, a medical doctor who knew I was writing this book, asked how it was coming along. As we discussed the importance of the subject, he shared (as I quoted in the introduction), "Well, it was about ten years ago that I finally came to terms with the negative effect my father had on me." His wife nodded affirmingly.

"Ten years ago?" I asked. "How old are you now?" This accomplished and successful man didn't come to terms with the damage caused by his father until he was in his mid-forties. "That's a long time to remain unresolved," I observed. "So...I assume you took everyone close to you along for the ride before coming to terms with it?" Robert's wife was once again visually affirming the answer to my question. Like many other men, Robert didn't look back until someone insisted that he get help for processing the ongoing effects of his past. I want to help men resolve things long before they reach their mid-forties.

Because far too many people connect their painful past to their fathers, I am calling men to let go of the pride that blinds them to the effects of past experiences. Be courageous and explore how your upbringing shaped the way you think, feel, and act in relationships. Be prepared, if necessary, to break with the past and pioneer a trail to a better future. If apologies should be involved, make them. Never minimize the empowering effect of asking a spouse or children for their forgiveness (no matter how old they are).

Five cautions for those with a painful past:

1. Remaining silent

Silence too often binds people to their past. Some choose to keep quiet about their past because they fear embarrassment and/or shame. Others remain silent because they don't know *how* or *where* to begin processing what they experienced. Yet silence only expands the effects of a troubled past and postpones dealing with those effects.

2. Self-absorbed introspection

When evaluating the effects of a painful upbringing, we can get stuck in self-absorbed introspection. The powerful allurements of self-pity, resentment, and bitterness accompany this temptation. We will explore those allurements more fully in chapter three.

3. Venting and lamenting

Processing feelings of loss and confronting suppressed emotions naturally lead to venting and lamenting. My caution here focuses more on remaining in a place of venting and lamenting, which then entices us to commiserate in the company of miserable people. Though you might experience superficial release from these choices, it's the wrong direction for those who desire to break the hold of the past.

4. Imagined versions of reality

Because children in dysfunctional homes tend to develop distorted views of reality, they become adults who struggle to perceive and assess the effects of their upbringing. The survival mechanisms of denial and suppression primarily cause these distorted realities. Children instinctively use denial and suppression as an emotional escape when actual escape is not possible. Since actual reality hurts too much, they nest in the safety of alternate realities, learning to deny their emotions and build walls around their hearts. Looking at life through the narrow lens of their dysfunctional homes, their reality is blurred.

Alternate realities easily become imagined or exaggerated versions of the past used to feed a victim mentality, draw sympathies of others, and protect cherished resentments. Accepting that we are victims of childhood trauma is necessary; a victim mentality, however, only promises to give extended life to the damage caused by others. Some won't let go of a victim mentality because they feel it gives them justified access to certain forms of redress (justice or vengeance).

5. Self-blame

An all-too-common alternate reality occurs when children accept responsibility for the hurtful actions of parents and other adults. Misreading what happens to them as an indication of something wrong with them, they place themselves at fault for being victimized. A woman in her early forties acknowledged that she finally began to overcome the effects of growing up in a violent home when she realized that what happened to her as a child was not her fault.

A grieving process toward a better future

This journey involves a grieving process that cycles through a variety of emotions. The way people work through these emotions will not be the same for everyone. Make allowance for unexpected waves of emotions but resist being trapped in any of them. Remind yourself often that you want to get to a better place. If we hope to resolve things in a healthy way, we must move beyond responses that multiply damage from the past. Ultimately, this book is an invitation to look back *so that you can move ahead.*

Buckle up for the ride

It might be wise to buckle up before reading this book. It could prove to be the ride of your life. Be patient in the process. Change takes time. Don't lose heart. Refuse to wave a towel of surrender to the past. Celebrate small victories on your way to a better future. The destination will be worth the journey!

Chapter 1: Evaluation and Discussion

1. Can you identify with any of the four typical reactions to a painful past (ignoring, denying, self-defeatedly accepting, perpetuating)?

2. What is the purpose of this book for someone who had a healthy upbringing?

3. Why did the author suggest that Diane was wrong in saying that men change after they get married?

4. Discuss ways that your past emerged in your adult relationships. Do you struggle with vulnerability, transparency and trust?

5. Why does the author give a particular challenge to men?

6. What did you find insightful or challenging from the stories of Charlie and Robert?

7. Were you able to identify with a specific caution for those with a painful past? Please explain.

Chapter 2

What good will it do to look back?

Perhaps you're not convinced about the need or value of examining your 18-year factor. I've met many people who realize that their upbringing continues to affect them but are unsure that looking back will accomplish anything. They usually express their hesitations with questions.

- "What good will it do to look back?"
- "Why revisit sad places from the past?"
- "If we can't change any of it, why bother going there?"
- "Why risk getting stuck in the past?"
- "Isn't it better to forget it and move on?"
- "Won't it just make me angrier and more resentful?"

Others are firmer in their opposition to visiting the past. They express their opposition in a variety of dismissive ways.

- "I let the past be the past."
- "I don't have time for dealing with my past."
- "I choose to focus on the positives."
- "I can't handle any more pain."
- "I have a right to feel the way I do about the past."
- "Some doors are better left unopened."

The questions and statements above seem like sensible approaches to a troubled past. After all, a desire to forget a sad memory is understandable. Rehearsing a painful experience seems like it could lead to resentment and bitterness. Why relive it? It's not my interest to cause anyone to revisit matters he or she prefers to forget. Nor do I desire to dig up resolved issues. The questions and statements above, however, are deflective clichés for *trying* to forget the past and for *denying* the ongoing effects.

Red flags tell us to look back when the effects of our past continue to reappear in our thoughts, feelings, and relationships. Suppressing and denying doesn't lead anyone to a better place. I've encountered far too many people who think they've put their past behind them even though it's disrupting their current lives and relationships.

While a guided look back is essential for overcoming damages caused during the first 18 years of life, it's especially important for protecting others. I always ask the man who tells me that he sees no value in looking back whether those who are close to him agree. "How is that working in your marriage?" I ask. The people living closely with someone who had a troubled past usually have a different opinion. Unresolved hurt from our upbringing comes with a risk of going through life hurting others—often without being aware of *how* and *why* we're doing it.

I don't want to think badly of my parents

Some people feel hesitant to revisit the past because of an instinct to defend parents—even when their parents are the primary cause of their past pain. They might offer any one of the following:

- "There are no perfect parents."
- "I guess my parents did the best job they could."
- "I don't think they meant to hurt me."
- "My father didn't exactly have a good home either."
- "I don't want to talk badly about them."

Although these statements probably originate from a desire to honor our parents, they deceptively minimize or dismiss the adverse effects of parents. The instinct to protect and defend parents is painfully evident in the following story.

Pick your parent day (Alex's story)

Alex, a man in his mid-thirties, sat across from me tearfully recalling the day his parents gave him a choice on the day they separated. In his words, "It was pick your parent day." When he was just nine years old, his parents asked, "Do you want to live with Mom or Dad?"

The backstory to this day was a home profoundly affected by his father's daily decision to either come directly home after leaving his high-profile professional job or (as was more typical) stop at the bar before returning home. "Dad was a functional alcoholic," Alex recalled. When his father drank too much, he became volatile and unpredictable. His dad often fought with his mother and was verbally and physically abusive to her. His parents decided to separate after a fight that ended with nine-year-old Alex aiming the family rifle at his dad's head, threatening to kill him if he didn't stop beating his mother. He will never forget that haunting moment of his life. How could he just put it behind him and forget it?

Alex's story took an unexpected turn when I asked him which parent he chose. He paused and looked down with tear-filled eyes as he admitted, "I chose to live with my dad." I was shocked. When I asked why he chose his dad, his answer was painfully incomprehensible to me. "I guess I just felt someone needed to look out for him." How is it possible that a nine-year-old boy felt a burden to look out for his abusive father? Isn't a father supposed to be the one who looks out for the well-being of his son? This man in his mid-thirties was still looking out for his manipulative, controlling and abusive father. I've repeatedly observed how this powerful instinct to protect a parent becomes disruptive to adult relationships.

Is it surprising that Alex struggles with personal and relational issues almost thirty years after his toxic upbringing? Telling him to "forget it and move on" would be both simplistic and dismissively hurtful. The same is true if someone suggested that there's no value in trying to understand the effects of childhood experiences.

Honoring parents

I respect a desire to honor parents. I also affirm the importance of sympathetically acknowledging the story behind your parents' story. Sorting out victims and perpetrators is not always as tidy as we might like it to be. Parents don't typically sit down and plot ways to harm their children. They parent their children out of the experiences of dysfunctional backstories.

We are wise to evaluate the effects our parents had on our lives with a willingness to see the positive as well as the negative from our upbringing. However, these balancing truths should not excuse or justify parents when they are responsible for damaging their children. A man once told me, "It wasn't until I almost lost my family that I knew I needed to come to terms with the damage my parents had done to me."

People from troubled upbringings who believe there's no value in looking back are superficially dismissing the effects their parents exerted upon them. This kind of response only blinds adults to the damage caused in their childhood years and binds the next generation to the impact. Personal and generational freedom from a painful past must include an honest and objective evaluation of the roles parents and other adults play in our upbringing; chapter four will focus on this evaluation.

Consider the following stories of two lives controlled by a father's verbal abuse long after the children left their homes. They offer a sobering reminder of the way a parent can send a child into a challenging future. First, you will meet Nora, a very kind woman whose life was dominated by self-doubt and self-rejection.

"My father always told me I was stupid" (Nora's story)

While living in northeast Philadelphia, I got to know Nora, an older lady who owned a little convenience store around the corner from our apartment. I noticed how kind she was to everyone she met, but I also heard her repeatedly put herself down. In normal conversation, she would say very negative things about herself. "I am not very smart." "I always mess things up." "This store will never be successful with me in charge."

Sometimes people say these things to get attention or to solicit praise and affirmation. However, Nora truly believed the negative words she spoke against herself. Furthermore, she also quickly deflected words of praise offered to counter her negative views of herself. Her words of self-deprecation conveyed the negative way she saw herself.

Finally, one day I asked Nora why she talked so negatively about herself. "What do you mean?" she asked. Sadly, she had spoken negatively about herself for so long that she was unaware of how it sounded. She replied that, although people often responded with compliments to counter her self-doubt, no one ever asked her why she talked badly about herself. Despite their good intentions, they didn't realize that her receptor for words of encouragement was far too damaged for her to benefit from them.

The damage done to Nora had a predictable story behind it. When I asked why she talked so negatively about herself, she paused and looked down at the floor.

I guess it goes back to the way my father treated me. He always told me that I was stupid and would never amount to anything. Whenever I did something wrong, he would angrily ask, "Why can't you get anything right?" and I guess after hearing these things for so long, I just believed that I'm stupid.

How sad to see Nora's life defined by the abusive words of her father. A father's voice should be one of the most encouraging ones a daughter hears. Didn't her father understand or care about the way his abusive words would wound his daughter's heart and send her into adult life imprisoned in self-doubt and feelings of worthlessness? Long after the experience of hearing her father's words, she continued to reaffirm his insults with her own words of self-deprecation. Parents send messages to their children that they subconsciously replay, which in turn shape the way they feel about themselves. For better or for worse, they possess the power to influence a child's future adult relationships significantly.

Nora lived without her father's affirmation and endured his constant verbal abuse throughout her childhood. Should we expect such abuse to result in long-lasting damage to her identity? How does an adult overcome this kind of childhood damage? And furthermore, how does this kind of damage affect adult relationships? Should we tell her to "just forget it and move on"? Should we tell her that her father didn't mean to hurt her? How would it help her if we told her to "just focus on positive things about herself?"

It's insensitive to expect that she could just hit an internal emotional switch and stop battling feelings of inferiority and inadequacy. Using superficial clichés about forgetting the past will likely only reaffirm her father's words in making her feel like more of a failure. Ask yourself how Nora would be a different person if her father had been (as fathers are meant to be) the safest and most encouraging man in her life? It's not difficult to imagine the answer. Lightly dismissing her lifelong battle devalues the importance of fatherhood.

Below, I will share a little about Jerry, one of my close boyhood friends. It's a reminder that some children respond in notably different ways to a father's verbal abuse.

31

"Where's that dummy son of mine?" (Jerry's story)

Jerry lived under a father who repeatedly degraded him. His favorite label for his son was "dummy." I saw the way his father treated him because I lived in his home for three months when my family moved. During that time, I never heard my friend's father use his proper name without attaching the label "dummy" to it. Most of the time, he only used the label "dummy" for my friend.

We laughed it off as children often do. We even mimicked his dad's label by calling each other dummy. Years later, however, I realized that there was nothing funny about his father's verbal abuse. What does it do to a boy when his dad (the most important man in a boy's life) repeatedly degrades him? Should we expect it to be left behind when he goes into adult life? Or, is it more likely that long after he leaves his home physically, he will remain attached in the way he thinks and feels about himself?

Jerry entered manhood not only deprived of his father's affirmation but deeply damaged from being the ongoing object of his father's verbal rejection. What does a father put in his son's heart by repeatedly calling him a dummy? Should we expect it to lead to feelings of insecurity and self-doubt? Would he privately become a bottomless pit of need for affirmation in a marriage relationship? Would years of abusing a boy's sense of worth and identity destroy his courage and confidence?

Jerry didn't appear to lack courage or confidence—*publicly*. His father's abusive words fueled a life-long mission to prove to the world that he's no dummy. As with many who suffered this way, however, Jerry lived between two people—his public confidence and his private insecurity.

Long after our boyhood years, Jerry had risen to a place of significant success and influence, and we got together to talk. After rehearsing boyhood memories and discussing where the years since those days had taken us, I led our conversation to another level. I requested permission to ask him a question. "Sure," he replied.

Looking into his eyes, I asked, "Have you done it yet? Have you accomplished your goal?"

With a puzzled look, he asked, "Done what?" After reminding him of my care for him as his friend, I asked him if he had proven to the world that he's no dummy.

The color left Jerry's face as he lowered his head and asked what I meant. I then suggested possible connections between his pursuit of success (and the way he spoke of his success) and his father's verbal abuse. It was disconcerting to observe that Jerry was unaware of the ways his father's verbal abuse shaped the direction of his life. How could the seemingly obvious connection with his painful past not be evident to him?

Exceptional stories?

I wish these stories were rare exceptions. Unfortunately, many people recall living without a father's affirmation and under his verbal abuse. It's sobering to discover how common it is for these people to be unaware of the impact parental neglect and abuse have on their current ways of thinking, the way they process emotions, and the troubles they experience in adult relationships. Looking back helps us see the connections from our past and how they exert a controlling influence over our lives.

Superficial clichés about forgetting the past become exposed for what they are when you walk with people who experienced a troubled and hurtful upbringing. Don't fall for these avoidance mechanisms. Denying the ongoing effects of our past and delaying the hard work of understanding how the influences affected us only ensures that more people will get hurt—especially spouses and children.

How we look back

The benefits of looking back will largely depend on how we approach it. If we look back to feed or to justify feelings of self-pity and resentment, we bind ourselves to the damage rather than moving toward a better future. Looking back is a beneficial process for the person who sincerely desires to understand *how* the past affects his life and *how to be free* from damaging adverse influences.

Chapter 2: Evaluation and Discussion

1. Why do people often question or oppose the value of looking back? What arguments do they typically give?

2. Why is it potentially hurtful to tell people to forget the past?

3. How might loyalty to parents hinder a willingness to look back?

4. What did you learn or find personally challenging from the stories about dysfunctional fathers (Alex, Nora, Jerry)?

5. Can you recall messages (positive or negative) that your parents sent to you about your identity?

6. What is the best way to look back?

Chapter 3

Toxic emotional drugs

Reacting to her upbringing in a violent home, Gina shared, "I escaped into the world of gambling, drugs, and alcohol—still trying to run from the terrors of abuse I experienced as a young child."

Gina is certainly not alone in using her addictions to mask the pain from her childhood years. Nonetheless, it's far more common for people to turn to *emotional drugs*—those enticing emotions that can dominate a person's life in reaction to a painful past. Like actual drugs, emotional drugs can become addictive in a way that makes users feel they cannot live without them. We must expose the risk of becoming attached to an emotional drug before we delve more closely into our 18-year factor.

Some of the more predictable emotional drugs include:

- resentment
- anger
- hatred
- bitterness
- self-pity
- self-loathing
- shame
- guilt
- fear

There's nothing unusual about a child from a troubled home experiencing these emotions; the danger is the temptation of becoming addicted to them in adult life.

Adults with painful upbringings carry with them a variety of emotions as a result. Sometimes these feelings come and go; other times they are blindsided with emotions when something triggers a reminder. When they form an unhealthy attachment to an emotional drug, they tend to justify their right to it because of how much they suffered. Pain lures us to believe that we deserve our addiction because it numbs our pain.

Emotional drugs (like actual drugs) offer superficial satisfaction and relief. When we can't get actual retaliation against the person(s) who hurt us, we substitute emotional revenge and derive a deceptive kind of satisfaction from it. The user of these drugs typically doesn't understand the way their emotional reaction extends the life of an abuser's damage. The critical difference is that the original abuser is not inflicting the damage. The victim switches roles and takes the abuser's part in damaging himself/herself through the emotional drug of choice. Consequently, the one who was hurt gives extended life to the abuser's damage by giving the abuser a controlling seat of influence in his/her heart. To put it another way, emotional drugs send an invitation to the one who hurt us to continue to poison our hearts. Emotional drugs multiply loss and spread damage to others—especially those close to the "user."

Blinded and bound to a past we hate

Raw emotional reactions are so often the chains that bind people to a painful past. Though emotions can deceptively feel like a means of escaping a painful past, they only send users into darker prisons of despair. We need to be very honest with ourselves about the emotional connections we make with a painful past. Likewise, we also need to reject the sense of entitlement we feel about our right to our emotional drug and the deceptive satisfaction it gives. We'll never experience freedom from the damaging effects of the past until we expose emotional drugs as extensions of the hurtful things done by others.

The story of a prisoner graphically illustrates the role of emotional drugs. During a question/answer session, he asked me what he should do with the hate he felt for his father.

"I hate my father so much" (Jim's story)

On a hot summer day, I was a guest speaker at the prison in our city. My theme was the 18-year factor. More than a hundred prisoners gathered in the commons, not to hear me necessarily, but to get out of their hot cells. The prison counselor asked me to speak for an hour and answer questions for twenty minutes. When I finished speaking, I asked if there were any questions. A prisoner named Jim raised his hand. "I have a question for you and you ain't gonna like the way I put it."

"Go ahead," I responded.

"My father called me a bum my whole life, and I got three boys on the outside who ain't ever gonna hear me call them a bum when I get out of here. But I hate my father so much that if he were on fire in front of me, I wouldn't waste my piss on him to put the fire out. Now, you tell me what I am supposed to do with that hate."

I walked closer to Jim and looked him directly in the eyes. "I'll tell you what. I'll answer your question if you answer mine." His eyes widened as I continued...

What are you going to let your hatred do to you and to everyone who gets close to you? Oh, you tell me you won't call your son a bum? I hope you're right but let me remind you that nothing good grows in a hate-filled heart!

Hate seems like the right response to a father who calls his son a bum his whole life. A man like that deserves to be hated, right? You can't get actual revenge, so you'll get emotional retaliation. Hate is your emotional drug of choice, and you feel you have a right to it. But what you don't seem to understand is that your hate is a means through which you give your father an extension on the damage he did to you.

If I slap you in the face, it's wrong. If YOU hit your face, it's stupid. It's no longer your father who is doing the damage to your life. You've taken over and continued to damage your life in reaction to him. You've invited your father to sit in your heart and poison it with an emotion that will make you toxic. Hatred always destroys the container that carries it. So I

40

want you to answer my question. What will you let your hate do to you and everyone who risks getting close to you?

I explained to Jim that *the only thing we can change about the past is the way it affects us in the future.* Freedom from the chains that hold us to our past requires an understanding of your emotional drug for what it is. Removing hatred from your heart will begin when you stop justifying it and using it to satisfy a desire for revenge. If you want to conquer hate, start by seeing it as an emotion that offers your father extended reach into your life. Think of your emotional drug of hate as a chain that binds you to the man who hurt you. Open your eyes to the real possibility of your hate spreading toxicity to others—especially to your sons.

Overcoming emotional drugs

Detoxing off an emotional drug requires a different understanding of it. Changing how we feel begins when we choose to think differently. Our brain places experiences in memory files that store the details of an experience, the emotions associated with it (anger, sadness, anxiety, fear, etc.), and the physiological responses it caused (muscle tension, increased blood pressure and respiration, to name a few).

To think differently about emotions, we must first attach to the memory file associated with the feelings a restraining truth: "My emotion is giving extended life to the words and actions of my abuser." Repeat this truth whenever something triggers remembrance of the way you were hurt. Gradually, this will expose the deceptive satisfaction of the emotion and counteract a tendency to justify your right to it. It will also force a reset in the way you recall and process painful memories.

We must not allow emotions to *bind* us to hurtful people and circumstances or *blind* us to the extended life our feelings give to damage caused by others. We empower ourselves to see things differently when we choose to view an emotional drug as an invitation to the one who hurt us to take a controlling seat in our hearts. Freedom comes when we unseat an abuser and make our emotions inaccessible to him/her.

An unforgiving heart

Many emotional drugs have connections with an unforgiving heart. Forgiveness is a complicated matter for significantly injured people. They feel a kind of pain that seems to have no pain-killer. However, the person who battles against bitterness knows that it's not easy to live well with an unforgiving heart. Suffering sometimes makes us feel self-justified entitlement to a kind of bitterness that becomes a cherished resentment. Yes, you read that correctly. *Cherished.*

Every time it feels right to remain unforgiving, counteract the feeling with this restraining truth: "Unforgiving hearts chain us to the one who hurt us and spread his damage to those who are close to us." Don't give an offender the power to keep hurting you long after he or she is gone.

"I refused to tie my soul to the one who hurt me"
(Kelly's story)

During a road trip, I was listening to a radio interview with Kelly, a woman who experienced sexual assault. As she spoke openly about her struggle to be free from anger and bitterness, she made a comment that was so significant it caused me to pull my car to the side of the road and write it down. She said that a critical step toward freedom from her abuser was getting to the place where, in her words, "I refused to tie my soul to the one who hurt me."

What a powerful way of describing a painfully difficult choice! She refused to allow her abuser to live in her soul and ruin her life. Her abuser was a thief who took control of part of her life, but she was determined not to allow him to extend his influence by sending her into years of anger and bitterness. This restraining truth was likely an ongoing reaffirmation until it became a way of thinking that unseated the abuser and made her emotions inaccessible to him.

Common emotional drugs

Look closely at some of the common emotional drugs of choice and be honest about the role they play in your life. Each one is an emotion that rules a heart in reaction to a painful past. Below, I've grouped them with feelings that share a commonality.

- Loss, regret, and self-pity
- Guilt, shame, and self-loathing
- Resentment, anger, and bitterness
- Hate, vindictiveness, and revenge
- Sadness, despair, hopelessness, and depression
- Fear, anxiety, and control

Chapter 3: Evaluation and Discussion

1. What is an emotional drug?

2. Describe the deceptive role of emotional drugs.

3. What did you find insightful or personally challenging from the stories of Gina, Jim, and Kelly?

4. What are some of the emotions you feel about your upbringing?

5. Can you identify with a specific dominant emotional reaction to your past?

6. What is essential for detoxing off an emotional drug?

7. What happens when our suffering from our past is left unchecked and unresolved?

EVALUATING THE PAST

How does the past affect the
present?

Introduction

Life is woven together with many threads of influence. Evaluating the effects of upbringing involves a closer look at how these influences shape a person's thoughts, feelings, beliefs, actions, and relationships. Under the primary influence of parents or guardians, children build their identity, security, and relationship skills.

When children become adults, they typically don't understand how childhood experiences connect with their lives. Revisiting your 18-year factor to evaluate the effects of your upbringing equips you to see and overcome unhealthy attachments to the past and to function well in adult relationships.

Let's begin the evaluation process with Lisa's painful story of what it was like for a little girl to live under a quiet, domineering father. Allow her courage in telling her story to cause you to begin to think deeply and talk openly about the effects of your 18-year factor as she did.

A quiet domineering father (Lisa's story)

I had a father who was very domineering in a quiet, controlled sort of way. He never hit us and very rarely yelled, but he would sit us down for lectures for hours during which we weren't allowed to speak, cry, or move a muscle. I learned early on how to turn myself off and wait it out because there wasn't any chance of changing anything. A lot of times he would have it wrong, or what he thought happened really didn't, but it didn't matter; we could never defend or explain, only sit and listen.

It was also well known that you never disagreed with him about anything—even a simple opinion. If he thought someone was mean, you darn well better agree, because if you said you didn't know they were that bad, you were in trouble. He was often quiet, but a stern look or gesture from him conveyed so much danger to me. I was always afraid of setting him off—even though he never hit us or anything like that. It seems difficult to understand how someone can rule with fear without actually doing anything. But I lived in fear of him.

My mother always deferred to his way. She never had her own opinion about anything—she'd learned not to. Dad's word was absolute law. And I pretty much always felt on the wrong side of the law, even though I was the "good child."

I was the oldest, so I took the role of doing whatever I can to make Dad happy. I had to be hyper-vigilant. I would carefully examine his body language, the feeling in the room—everything—and choose my every word and gesture and facial tic so that Dad would like what I said. If I used the wrong word, I'd hear about it for the next several hours. I got good at reading him. I knew the topics that he liked to discuss, and what tone of voice to use and everything. It became a survival mechanism for life in my home.

My sister went with a different approach. She gave up. She rebelled and did everything consciously opposite to what was expected (I guess she partly did this because I'd already claimed the "good girl" role of the family). She is still doing this well into her adult life and has no idea why.

The problem for me came in that I had no idea at the time that this wasn't normal. I thought that what I experienced was in the scope of normal family relations, and never once thought of it as dysfunctional. So that made it harder for me to fix. My sister now has this problem because she doesn't remember it as damaging.

After I got married and we had a disagreement, I'd immediately shut down and tried to "wait it out" like I always did with Dad. It was a physical thing. I could not make myself talk to my husband and sort out a disagreement in a calm way. In my experience, you didn't disagree; you kept it inside and waited until it was over. For the first year of marriage, our disagreements were over small things, but they became long, drawn-out affairs in which my husband tried for hours to get me to talk.

Fortunately for me, I have a husband who loves me dearly and can't stand to be in a disagreement with me, so he wouldn't let me retreat. He'd keep at it until it was solved, and I finally realized that I was hurting him by doing what I was doing. I made conscious efforts to change, but it was difficult for me. I had to physically force myself to look at him, say something—anything—at first.

Eleven years later, we're much better at arguing. One of us will say what's bothering us, and we'll talk about it like healthy people. No more five-hour-long standoffs— but I had to choose it. I could have easily let it ruin a wonderful relationship.

Relationship damage

The other legacy from my childhood is my tendency to hyper-analyze people. I look at all the nonverbal cues in a room and am very sensitive to anyone seeming to be put off by me. My body screams "Danger! Danger!" when I hear a tone of voice or see body language that shows there's an argument coming, or anger, or anything.

Usually, those cues don't mean anything—or, at least not anything that should worry me. I have had to learn that it's okay to disagree with people or have people not like what I say, as long as I do my part with love. I've also had to learn that very little I see has to do with me, and that a lot of times I see danger where there's absolutely nothing.

My husband said to me, "Honey, no one else does that. No one else sees these things or looks for them. It's just you." It sounds simple, but I hadn't seen it that way before. Learning to stop over-analyzing has helped me have more normal, less intense relationships with people. I had started to do what Dad always had done: want people to agree with me all the time, because if not they were "against" me. Not surprisingly, my father's father was even more like that than my father, so it's a family legacy. One that I've cut short.

Even with being in a much better place than I used to be, I still find relationships exhausting. It wears me out when I have too much social interaction. A result of my dysfunctional upbringing that is difficult is my need to limit the number of close relationships in my life.

Identity damage

I also have a hard time knowing what about me is a flaw from my childhood that I should change, and what is just "me." I'm very much an introvert. I live in my head and get energy from solitude. Is this a legacy from my father, or just me being me? Is it okay for me to embrace that part of my personality, or is it something I'm supposed to change? Sorting out the difference is sometimes hard and exhausting for me.

New people needed

My husband is the exact antidote to my father. He is self-sacrificing, open, affectionate, and understanding. He doesn't let me get away with being removed or difficult. He loves me and makes sure I know it. Not many women can say that.

Before continuing with Lisa's story, we should note that the emotional drug of embarrassment/shame about a painful past tempts people to conceal it from potential mates. Fear of being rejected as "damaged goods" is powerful. It's far better, however, to make the past known before marriage. Understanding Lisa's past protected her husband from misreading the effects when they resurfaced in marriage. Her husband would have likely interpreted Lisa's behaviors as personal affronts against himself if he had not known the story behind her story. The role he took in helping Lisa overcome her past is a needed example for husbands and wives.

Back to Lisa's story...

Survival mechanisms

I learned how to shut down during my father's lectures and carried this into my adult life, especially my marriage. When I say I would shut down during arguments with my husband, I mean I completely shut down. I'd lie in bed (since it was usually at night) facing away from him, closing my eyes, not speaking. I felt nothing—literally nothing. Not fear or sadness or love. I was empty and waiting for it to end. I usually said things in my head that I would say if I were speaking, but I never said them out loud. I always did this when I was young too.

My husband would beg me to look at him, talk to him, telling me that he is my husband and that he loves me and asking why I wouldn't talk to him. He'd even cry and plead with me, but I was unmoved. That's how shut-off I was.

I felt absolutely nothing during standoffs with Dad. Shutting down was the only way of getting through Dad's lectures without crying or arguing. I learned to be stoic like he wanted me to be. But it was horrible when it carried over into my marriage. And I didn't know how to change. One night my husband was begging me to turn around and look at him...

We'll come back to Lisa's story later.

The power entrusted to parents

Lisa's story reveals the kind of damage dysfunctional parents do to their children. Imagine what it was like for this little girl to navigate her life around such a dysfunctional father. Unaware and unconcerned about how he was damaging his daughter, he tore down her sense of identity and her feelings of security. Through his manipulation, he set her up for a future of self-doubt and unresolved issues. Her story is a sobering reminder of how much power one adult has to send another human being into a difficult life.

The insights and guidance I share in this book played a role in sparing Lisa from what could have been many more years of pain and suffering.

Chapter 4

Primary Influences: Relationships

When evaluating how upbringing affects life, specific focus should be given to three primary influences: *relationships*, *circumstances*, and *physical challenges*. We begin life nested in a web of relationships that play an important role in shaping us. Parents are the *primary relationship* that affects the 18-year factor.

Circumstances and *physical challenges* during childhood years also exert life-changing influences. Circumstances include things that happened to and around us that had life-altering effects. Physical challenges include aspects of our appearance or physical limitations that made us feel different, insecure, or targeted for ridicule. Children do not respond in the same way to these influences. Indeed, siblings who experience a dysfunctional home often respond differently to their upbringing. Differences in temperaments play a role in forming reactions to the primary influences of childhood years.

Relationships

Lisa's story involved a quiet domineering father who not only failed to store up good things in the treasure chest of her heart but made many destructive deposits that caused damaging influences well beyond her childhood years. The harm he caused explained a lot about the way she approached relationships. Nora (who owned the convenience store) and Jimmy (my boyhood friend) were also profoundly affected by harmful deposits from their fathers. These dysfunctional fathers remained seated in the control room of their hearts long beyond their childhood years.

The influence of parents, of course, is not always damaging. Others recall very encouraging words from their parents. These adults were raised in one of the diminishing number of healthy homes in our communities. They draw from the good messages deposited in their hearts that contributed to a healthy self-understanding and a stabilizing sense of security and confidence.

When our anchor is hooked to a healthy foundation, we meet the trials and challenges of life with strength and stability. Those who didn't experience this kind of upbringing feel they have no safe place to put their anchor when the storms hit.

Making connections

Connections between the past and present commonly emerge in counseling sessions when someone says, "I guess it all goes back to my father...." or, "With how my mother treated me, I shouldn't be surprised..." or "My father wasn't a very kind person." The way our parents related with us and spoke to us during our upbringing stored messages and emotions in our hearts. These messages and emotions transfer through words, tones of voice, actions, and examples of parents and other adults. The messages then shape the way we think and feel about our value and worth as well as our overall opinion of ourselves. They also play a decisive role in the way we approach relationships.

The extent of influence upbringing exerts is not the same for everyone. All people, however, benefit from connecting the lines between their 18-year factor and their current sense of identity, way of processing emotions, and approach to adult relationships. The need for a closer look at these influences is an especially urgent matter for those who grew up in dysfunctional homes.

Active and passive ways parents affect children

Looking back at the life-affecting roles of our parents, guardians or other adults requires an understanding of active and passive ways they affect us. Dysfunctional parents *actively* perpetrate damage on their children (through abuse) and *passively* deprive them of a healthy upbringing (through neglect).

Perpetration (abuse) and Deprivation (neglect)

The stories from previous chapters revealed the damaging effects of parental *perpetration* through abusive treatment and words. Perpetration (active abuse), however, is not the only way parents hurt their children. It's equally common for children to suffer under parental *deprivation* (neglect). Perpetration and deprivation rarely exist without each other, but it helps to look through the lens of each one. Parents who deprive their children of consistent, loving discipline and mature guidance send them into adult life unprepared for its challenges and temptations. Various forms of parental deprivation are often the story behind adult feelings of insecurity and vulnerability.

Cavities and cravings

Sending harmful verbal messages to a child is not the only way parents cause damage. A father who withholds affection and acceptance from his daughter leaves deep cavities and intense cravings in her heart. He is responsible for the unstable environment that deprived her of security and confidence needed for adult life. It's not unusual for a child who comes from this kind of home to spend years multiplying pain and trying to fill the voids left by a dysfunctional parent.

A narrow and limited future

Neglectful parents leave cavities and cravings in a child's heart, but they also narrow the lens through which a child views the future. Dysfunctional parents often cause a child to be unable to see the potential of an open future. Painful childhood experiences sometimes lead to a kind of short-sightedness—a myopic condition of the heart that disproportionately defines the future based on a painful past. Hurtful parents are often the story behind adults who nest in the perceived safety of a limited life. These adults react to their past by choosing unimaginative, unadventurous and uncreative lives. Fear of risking more hurt and suffering that they experienced in one part of their lives disincentivizes them throughout the rest of their lives. In this case, we need courage to refuse to allow a piece of our past to disproportionately and unrealistically control and limit our future.

For example, a young lady might choose to avoid male relationships because her violent father caused her to believe that all men become violent. A boy might become a man who chooses a low-risk life of limited potential because of many years of experiencing tensions and fighting between his parents whenever finances were tight. The continuing need to cheer up a depressed mother might cause a young man to become too easily dispirited or unrealistically opposed to anything negative. The child who continually feels a need to mediate and calm her quarreling parents might choose to avoid all confrontation in her adult life—despite the damaging effect on her future relationships.

What my life could have been... (Stephanie's story)

Stephanie, a mother with a successful career in the medical field, acknowledged that she often wonders what her life could have been had she grown up in a normal home.

What else could I have accomplished if my confidence in my own abilities had not been challenged and damaged at such a young age and to such a hurtful degree? I will not ever know what could have happened. All I can do is understand that when I was young, instead of being nurtured in times when normally a lesson could have been learned, I was physically beaten and run down with words of hatred. This created emotions and feelings that I was unable to understand. I went out into life unprepared for the realities that exist in everyday living.

One or two adults can place powerful default settings in a child's heart—settings for how she thinks, feels, and relates to others. We must be honest about ways we remain under the control of those who hurt us long after we leave their actual presence. Gaining freedom requires a resolute decision not to allow dysfunctional adults to write the script for the future.

How I view myself

Evaluating the 18-year factor requires honesty about the negative messages and emotions planted in our hearts during this impressionable and formative time. Identifying your primary opinions and feelings about yourself is crucial for enjoying healthy adult relationships, though we cannot attribute these messages and emotions solely to the effect of parents. They are formed through a convergence of parental influence, circumstantial factors, and physical challenges. Additionally, differences in personality and temperament also affect our self-beliefs. Therefore, it's helpful to identify the role each contributes in shaping the opinions and emotions behind the way we view ourselves.

My parents made me feel...

Since our upbringing shapes our sense of personal identity (for better or worse) under the primary influence of parents and other adults, a helpful way to assess the ongoing effects is to finish the line, "My parents made me feel..." What are the messages and emotions that your parents stored in your heart? Consider some of the responses I've heard.

- My parents made me feel worthless, like I was meant to be a failure.
- My parents always cast doubt on my potential.
- My father was unsympathetic toward my feelings.
- My parents used shame and guilt to manipulate me.
- My father created an atmosphere of fear and unpredictability with verbal threats.
- My mother created tensions through extreme mood swings.
- My parents made me feel that my opinions and thoughts didn't matter.
- My father belittled me and used minimizing, mocking, condescending tones.
- I lived with significant ongoing tension between parents.

After we look more closely at how our parents made us feel, we need to then ask how we continue to feel about ourselves.

Consider some of the negative and positive words/labels below. Although we might occasionally identify with many of these words, I am interested in identifying the words associated with frequently recurring feelings that play a significant role in the way we see ourselves.

Negatives

Violated, uncertain, ashamed, unloved, distrustful, betrayed, awkward, unaccepted, self-loathing, angry, stupid, a failure, hopeless, bitter, dirty, fearful, defiled, unworthy, confused, resentful, guilty, powerless, degraded, anxious, helpless, unstable, aimless, depressed, rejected, condemned, lonely, discontented, uneasy, valueless, craving acceptance and affirmation, negative, in bondage, unwanted, weak, vulnerable, phony, pessimistic, different, dark, etc.

Positives

Safe, loved, secure, hopeful, stable, clean, balanced, accepted, peaceful, content, purposeful, free, forgiven, capable, smart, trustful, courageous, affirmed, worthy, meaningful, encouraged, supported, confident, discerning, humble, merciful, determined, self-assured, forgiving, compassionate, talented, appreciated, skillful, wise, joyful, etc.

Minimize the costs

We can minimize the personal and relational costs of remaining attached to painful childhood experiences (and the protective mechanisms that go with them) by first discovering and examining the causal pathways that led to them. It's difficult to forget what you don't understand, just as it's difficult to know how the past continues to affect your present without a better understanding of it.

Counteract negative messages and labels

Changing how we think and feel about ourselves requires determination and new ways of thinking. We cannot *feel* differently without first choosing to *think* differently.

Memory files

As mentioned in chapter three, it helps to understand how our brains store memory files of the details of painful or traumatic experiences along with the physical and emotional responses to them. When something triggers a reminder of a painful experience (especially regarding our parents), our brains pull up the memory file and send us back through the thoughts, feelings, and even physical responses related to the painful or traumatic experience.

For example, if you carry painful memories about a father or mother, the holidays of Father's Day and Mother's Day can trigger bad memories that usher in a correlating negative mood. Similarly, and more tragically, a friend of mine (at the vulnerable age of 15), discovered his father who had just committed suicide on a day in October. Each October after that traumatic experience, a dark cloud came over my friend's life. At the encouragement of his wife, he finally sought counseling to process and overcome the effects of this experience.

Overcoming painful past experiences always requires counteractive truths. These truths must be inserted in the memory file (like antivirus software) to combat the adverse effects of recalling the past. My friend could start with the counteractive truth that resolving the pain of the past is a movement beyond responses that *extend* and *multiply* the damage. Refusing to make himself responsible for his father's death is another counteractive truth. It should help us to redirect our thinking when we see how we are causing others to suffer from our unhealthy attachment to a traumatic experience.

It's time to leave home

Far too many adults physically leave their homes but continue to live in them emotionally and psychologically. **Daring to**

63

completely leave home requires courage, determination, and a decisive plan. In the last section of the book, I outline a proposal for a better future—a plan for unseating abusive people from the control room of the heart. Before considering this plan, however, other steps for evaluating the 18-year factor must be followed. The life-altering roles of childhood *circumstances* and *physical challenges* should receive closer inspection.

Chapter 4: Evaluation and Discussion

1. What did you find insightful or helpful from Lisa's story in the Introduction?

2. What are the three primary influences to consider in evaluating upbringing?

3. Can you identify ways in which the influence of parents or other adults continues to affect your thoughts, feelings, beliefs, actions, or adult relationships?

4. What messages did your parents send to you about your identity/intelligence/appearance/value/ability?

5. What are your thoughts about the way the past limits and narrows the future?

6. What are the possible reasons why many people identify with Stephanie's story?

7. How would you finish the line, "My parents made me feel _____"?

8. What is your response to the suggested role of memory files?

9. Have you left home completely, or do you have unhealthy attachments?

Chapter 5

Primary influences: circumstances and physical challenges

Let's take a closer look at the roles of circumstances and physical challenges during our 18-year factor. Circumstances from childhood years can explain much about the way we think, feel and act as adults—including ways teachers or peers mistreated us or the effects of unstable circumstances. By the same token, physical challenges during our 18-year factor also shape the way we see ourselves. Being repeatedly ridiculed as a child because of physical appearance or physical disabilities and limitations fall in this category. When children feel rejected because of things that make them different (but cannot be changed), the effects do not end when they reach adulthood.

The role of circumstances

The circumstances of our childhood years are the stage or setting for the movie of our lives. Evaluating the way upbringing affects life includes a journey back to the circumstances of our 18-year factor. Specific parts of my own life circumstances might provide helpful examples.

My life circumstances

I was the oldest son and second oldest child in a family of eleven children. Consequently, I had to help much more with family needs. I vividly recall many financial pressures due to the needs of such a large family. On a number of occasions, we were uncertain whether our family would have adequate food to eat. At a young age, I cut a lot of firewood because we couldn't always afford oil to heat our house. When I was about ten years old, our financial pressures intensified. My father was struck with a severe case of rheumatism that affected his ability to work. Watching my dad suffer was an ongoing part of the setting for my life. It also increased my sense of responsibility to help with family needs. I often tried to think of ways I could make money to help our family, though my options were limited by my young age. This led to an internal battle with feelings of helplessness and hopelessness.

Increased financial difficulties played a role in our moving to different homes on nine occasions. This added to my life the challenge of adjusting often to being the new kid in school and neighborhood. An additional reality further exacerbated my adjustments; my surname during my childhood years was "Butts." It was like a very clear target on my back for many of my peers to ridicule me. Years later I changed our last name from "Butts" to "Cornell" (my wife's maiden name) to protect our children from ridicule. Frequently moving made me feel increasingly alone and outside of the accepted group. It also contributed to my battles with learning disabilities and gave me a feeling of never measuring up.

When I was 15 years old, my life veered off in a negative direction. Our family moved to northeast Philadelphia and I got mixed up with a bad crowd. Some of the cumulative effects of my circumstantial challenges caught up with me. I began to emotionally shut down and rebel against anyone who tried to tell me how to live. I stopped caring and became increasingly angry. Rather than trying to do well in school work, I belittled the need for school and scoffed at "the worthless stuff" we were required to learn. Rather than trying to be accepted, I acted like I didn't need anyone. This was my protective mechanism for handling the pressures of life.

Temperament makes a difference

Considered the natural or genetic part of personality, temperament plays a role in how circumstances affect us. I inherited my temperament from my German-Irish father by nature and nurture. There was nothing passive or shy about his temperament. If I had a different temperament, my experiences would have likely caused much more social anxiety. I wasn't the kind of child who patiently endured mistreatment. When ridiculed for my last name, I came out with both fists swinging, never surrendering my outward confidence even when I lacked good reason for it. I suppressed feelings of insecurity and fear under the power of a strong personality.

My parents believed I was destined to be a leader. They were right. But before leading anything good, I became a leader on the streets of Philadelphia. At 16, I left my home to run with gangs. My high school disciplinarians finally gave up on me and asked me to leave the school. I am grateful that where I've been didn't define who I've become.

Positive influences

Despite being a "bad street kid," I had a soft spot for disadvantaged people. If I witnessed anyone mistreating the handicapped or the elderly, I quickly put an end to it by inviting him to harm me instead. When they wisely decided not to take my offer, I followed with a threat to hurt them if they did it again. This part of my narrative had a story behind it. Before leaving my home, I lived with my grandmother for about nine months. She was very kind to me. My mentally disabled cousin also lived in the house, and I cared for him very much. My love and respect for both of them likely explain the way I defended people I viewed as disadvantaged.

Connecting childhood circumstances with adult life

The consistent presence of loving parents significantly minimized the adverse consequences of my childhood circumstances. My father's courageous acceptance of suffering (without complaint) also had a strong positive influence on my life.

As I examine my adult life, however, I recognize negative ways I think and process emotions that connect with childhood circumstances. Financial challenges trigger unnecessary fears. I battle feelings of hopelessness when I feel helpless to change things. Often feeling alone and not part of the "accepted" group (due partly to my temperament), I reacted by becoming more independent to protect myself from needing people. Although some of the consequences of this reaction prepared me for a life of senior leadership, I had to overcome other effects that conflicted with team leadership.

Watching my father suffer through the years magnifies the stress I feel when I see someone I love suffering. Feeling that it was unfair for my parents to struggle so much makes it difficult for me to see people endure disproportionate struggles. Justice issues have always been a challenge for me. Regrets over lost parts of my life in Philadelphia occasionally cause me to battle thoughts of how my life could have been better if I had not experienced the problematic circumstances of my 18-year factor.

Technical names

Obviously, challenging circumstances of childhood years are not the same for everyone. Yet my adult reactions to childhood circumstances share some typical characteristics with the way others react. A number of technical names are given to these characteristics.

- *Cognitive glitches*—our thinking triggers and fixates disproportionately and unrealistically because of painful past experiences.
- *Attribution bias*—we attribute threats to situations that remind us of part of our past but are actually harmless and neutral.

- *Dysregulated flight-or-fight*—our internal system for regulating responses unnecessarily and quickly goes into flight or fight mode because of part of our past. Flight mode is an escape into sullenness and silence. Fight mode is expressed with angry and rash reactions.[1]

An important choice

The choice not to allow the past to define who I am but to include it in who I become has helped me process negative effects from childhood circumstances. As a result, I can affirm the positive and valuable life lessons that arose from my experiences. On the positive side, I see how difficulties from my upbringing prepared me for helping others process the effects of a painful past. It's my hope that transparency about my own challenges will inspire others to look at the role circumstances played in developing their current feelings about themselves and the ways they think and act as adults.

Physical challenges

The same honest assessment of circumstances must also be applied to the physical challenges that were part of our 18-year factor. Before considering specific and unique physical challenges, though, it's helpful to review the typical challenges of growing from adolescence to adulthood. This part of the journey of life comes with a number of relatively common physical, emotional and psychological challenges.

Growth from adolescence to adulthood

Undoubtedly, puberty is a tumultuous journey. Normal physical changes during this phase cause personal awkwardness and social stress for young people. When boys enter what has been called "the awkward stage," sometimes their body parts appear to be oddly assembled. They commonly experience changes in their voices, growth of facial/body hair, and undesirable bodily odors. Emerging interest in sexuality causes personal and social challenges. At the same time, girls often feel awkward about their body image, bodily changes, and their menstrual cycle. A struggle with acne is another common cause of stress during this phase of life.

Common experiences

The pre-teen and teen years typically place children in a variety of tunnels. They spend time in *the tunnel of confusion* where they feel conflicted over emerging adult and lingering childhood interests and desires. They experience *the tunnel of emotion* where they feel an array of spontaneous and often irrational mood swings: from happy and excited, to sad and depressed, to agitated and angry. *The tunnel of self-consciousness* cycles them through a sense of inferiority and feelings of rejection to a sense of superiority and feelings of acceptance. Puberty contributes to the tunnel of self-consciousness with experiences that make them feel anywhere from simply awkward to downright weird.

The *tunnel of hormones* is another challenge—a place filled with swirling experiences of raging and unpredictable desires combined with a variety of irrational and extreme mood swings. Sometimes a surge of confidence emboldens them to test their sense of independence. However, confidence can quickly dissipate as feelings of self-doubt replace it. Then there's *the tunnel of sexual desire* where they are conflicted between awkward but intense interest in sex and guilt for being interested.

Parental overreactions to these normal parts of the physical and emotional journey from adolescence to adulthood only make life more difficult for everyone. Both parents and children benefit from repeated reminders not to overreact to the changes and challenges of this phase of life. On the other hand, parents must equally be careful not to underreact by withholding the encouragement and guidance young people need for this part of their journey.

Unique physical challenges

Beyond the common experiences we all share as we grow into adults, unique physical challenges can be life-altering during the formative 18-year factor. A teenage friend of mine struggled with a severe case of stuttering that repeatedly caused social awkwardness for him. Another friend had a stub instead of his right arm. Without harmful intent, we nicknamed him "Stubs." No one ever thought to ask how he felt about that name.

Children with excess weight are painfully aware when people stare at them, make comments about their appearance, or ask insensitive questions. These children often become victims of appearance bullying. Other children feel negatively about themselves because they lack athletic ability. They know how it feels to always be chosen last for a team or to never win a ribbon on track and field day. Telling these children that we're all winners won't help them. They're too smart to fall for artificial forms of encouragement that are designed more to make adults feel better than to help children.

Understandably, appearance issues and physical limitations can be personally and socially traumatic for children. Parents sometimes make matters worse by being notably indifferent to a child's struggle. While it's important to help children learn to accept themselves and even to laugh at themselves, we dare not minimize the harmful ways these ongoing experiences shape a child's sense of identity. A child who battles intensified feelings of self-consciousness can gradually develop harmful feelings of self-loathing and self-rejection. This emotional cycle significantly damages a child who is repeatedly victimized by appearance bullying.

Damage to a vital internal receptor

Struggles with physical limitations and disabilities during childhood years make adult relationships difficult in ways that are not widely understood. Children who endure these struggles without loving and attentive parents especially need help in processing their emotions and building a secure and healthy identity. Without help, relationship difficulties arise from damage done to a vital internal receptor. This receptor allows us to beneficially process criticisms and genuinely accept compliments. When children are repeatedly singled out and ridiculed for their physical appearance, it damages this vital internal receptor for beneficial relationships.

The protective mechanisms used for enduring the abuse also damage this internal receptor. Children protect themselves by emotionally shutting down or by suppressing and denying their painful feelings. To limit the risks that accompany social interaction, they build walls around themselves. Since they don't believe compliments (especially those about their appearance), they cannot benefit from them. They unfairly project their feelings of self-loathing and self-rejection onto others, living with deflective resistance to criticism—even from people who love them. Because their internal receptor was overloaded by abusive people who repeatedly ridiculed them, they cannot benefit from healthy self-criticism.

Sometimes an adult who endured this kind of childhood abuse finds it difficult to admit to being wrong and rarely speaks the beneficial words, "I am sorry." They deflect things that imply something wrong about themselves and redirect blame on others. Unfortunately, they cannot benefit from being sorry *about* themselves because they are consumed with being sorry *for* themselves. Though the protective mechanism of self-pity guards them from self-loathing, it also deprives them of the benefits of an examined life.

Undeniably, close relationships are difficult for those who were abused. Along with the walls they build around themselves, they sometimes assign blame for the damage done in the past to those who are close to them. They push people away by rejecting compliments as disingenuous and resisting constructive criticism. As a result, they tend to make others unsure if it's possible to love them in a normal way. The needed qualities for meaningful relationships (vulnerability, transparency, and trust) are inaccessible because of the risk of more hurt.

Gaining an understanding of the damage done to this vital internal receptor and the nature of the extended consequences has been helpful to many people. The matter of restoring the receptor is something I'll address in the final section of the book.

Closer evaluation is needed if the three influences of relationships, circumstances and physical challenges rise to the categories of a *significant disruptions* or a *severe dysfunctions*. In the next two chapters we will focus on these categories.

Chapter 5: Evaluation and Discussion

1. Describe (if any) the challenging circumstances you experienced in your 18-year factor.

2. Do you recognize any extensions from your childhood circumstances in your adult life? Explain.

3. Summarize the important choice that the author made in overcoming the adverse effects of his childhood circumstances.

4. Describe some of the positive results that came from the circumstances of your 18-year factor.

5. Do you recall specific challenges from adolescence to adulthood? Explain.

6. Share any specific physical challenges you experienced during your childhood years.

7. Did you or someone you know suffer from appearance bullying?

8. Summarize the effects of damage done to the vital internal receptor.

Chapter 6

Significant Disruptions

The life-altering effects of disruptive and dysfunctional childhood experience profoundly affect the way we think, feel, and act in adult life. Enjoying healthy adult relationships will depend on how well we process these experiences.

Children feel helpless and hopeless when traumatic experiences significantly disrupt the most formative years of life. They lose their sense of safety and security. Home feels like an unstable place. Such disruptions could include divorce/separation from parents, physical or sexual abuse, domestic violence, incarceration of a parent, death of a loved one, or a severe illness. In this chapter, we will consider a few of these.

The day my childhood ended

The most common disruption of the 18-year factor is the separation and divorce of one's parents. In the prior chapter, I noted that the challenges of my own personal childhood circumstances were significantly minimized by the consistent presence of loving parents. In contrast, one adult child of divorce (ACOD) looked back on the traumatic experience of his parents' separation and divorce and remarked, "The day my parents divorced was the day my childhood ended." His parents' divorce ended his sense of childhood innocence and forced him to process adult emotions far beyond his maturity.

People entertain many myths about the effects of divorce on children. Some adults, (wanting to divorce but feeling guilty about the possible impact on their children), argue that children are resilient and will soon get over the stress of divorce. This is a myth. The divorce of parents is not simply a temporary trauma that only exerts its harmful effects on children at the time of their parents' breakup.

The jury returned with the verdict

The jury has returned to the courtroom with a united verdict regarding the adverse effects of divorce on children. The evidence is undeniable. In her well-documented book, *The Unexpected Legacy of Divorce*, Judith Wallerstein followed the lives of more than a hundred children for 25 years from the time of their parents' divorce into their own adulthood experiences. The jury of these adult children of divorce returned with a verdict that exposes the myths.

Wallerstein focused on seven of those who characterized the collective experiences of the larger group. The study exposed two myths: that ending an unhappy marriage is better for the children, and that if the parents are happier after a divorce, the children will be happier too.

Adult children of divorce are telling us loud and clear that their parents' anger at the time of the breakup is not what matters most. Unless there was violence or abuse or unremitting high conflict, they have dim memories of what transpired during this supposedly critical period...

It's the many years living in a post-divorce or remarried family that count, according to this first generation to come of age and tell us their experience.

It's feeling sad, lonely, and angry during childhood. It's traveling on airplanes alone when you're seven to visit your parent. It's having no choice about how you spend your time and feeling like a second-class citizen compared with your friends in intact families who have some say about how they spend their weekends and their vacations. It's wondering whether you will have any financial help for college from your college-educated father, given that he has no obligation to pay.

It's worrying about your mom and dad for years—will her new boyfriend stick around, will his new wife welcome you into her home? It's reaching adulthood with acute anxiety. Will you ever find a faithful woman to love you? Will you find a man you can trust? Or will your relationships fail just like your parents' relationship did? And most tellingly, it's asking if you can protect your own child from having these same experiences in growing up.[1]

Wallerstein warns readers that the popular myths about the effects of divorce have "prevented us from giving children and adults the understanding they need to cope with the divorce experience over the long haul."

Sexual abuse

Turn out the light in your eyes

In a television show a few years ago, a female police officer preparing to go undercover as a prostitute had an exchange with an actual prostitute as part of her preparation for the assignment. The prostitute approached the officer and got close to her face and asked her if "her daddy ever touched her when she was a little girl."

The prostitute then got even closer. She looked into the eyes of the officer for an uncomfortable amount of time and said, "Turn the light off in your eyes." The officer understood what she meant and tried to make her eyes appear to be empty and hopeless.

What a sad but realistic way to describe the emotionless expression of someone who had been sexually violated. What does it look like when the light is turned off in someone's eyes? These are eyes void of light. They are eyes that tell us that there's a story behind the story.

Sexual abuse is another sadly common disruption of an 18-year factor. Although victims of sexual abuse often feel very alone in their suffering, according to the United States Department of Health and Human Services, a child is sexually assaulted in the U.S. every eight minutes, and 93 percent know the perpetrator.[2] Many perpetrators of sexual abuse are in a position of trust or responsibility for the child's care, such as a family member, teacher, clergy or coach.[3]

Several years before my first encounter with a victim of sexual abuse, I took a graduate course in psychology that included a significant focus on sexual abuse. I was naively frustrated about the requirement to focus so much on sexual abuse. Since I knew little about sexual abuse, I didn't think I would encounter the issue very often. I was wrong.

Over the following decades, I counseled more people dealing with a history of sexual abuse than I could have imagined. The class focus played an important role in equipping me to assist many people who were struggling to overcome the life-debilitating effects of sexual abuse. My eyes opened to a world of darkness that holds its victims in silent pain. My heart grew heavy for the victims of such evil.

Most of my counseling has focused on those who were sexually abused as children by an extended family member. They came to me as adults who are struggling to live normal lives. Not surprisingly, victims battle feelings of helplessness and hopelessness. Because their abuse included manipulation and force, they long for a sense of security and control. Fear drives them to controllable behaviors as they try to gain a feeling of being in control of their lives. Extreme exercise and dieting are two examples. Yet gaining control only becomes an elusive dream as feelings of powerlessness and an inability to function inexplicably overwhelm them. As a result, they spiral in and out of cycles of despair.

They suffer in the pain of silence. Whom can they turn to for help? Who will believe them? Maybe people will think they're defiled and dirty. Maybe their perpetrator was right when he accused them of bringing it on themselves. Perhaps those who hear about their abuse will never consider them to be normal.

It's not unusual for survivors to experience significant loneliness, loss of appetite and need for abnormal amounts of sleep. Mood swings also plague those battling the grip of sexual abuse. Unusual gregariousness can give way to unexplainable depression and crying. Other waves of emotion include self-hatred, panic attacks, irrational phobias, guilt, shame, an overall sense of humiliation, unexplained anger and rage, lack of normalcy and a feeling of being trapped.

Survivors of sexual abuse sometimes turn to other forms of abuse to escape their pain. Obsessive behaviors range from alcohol and drug abuse to sexual addictions and promiscuity. Sometimes victims engage in self-mutilation and battle suicidal thoughts.

A caring friend is needed, but...

Most victims of sexual abuse don't understand how badly they've been affected. They suppress the past to survive the present. Victims often try to conceal their pain and keep others at a superficial distance. Without the help of a caring friend, victims of sexual abuse will suffer in silence for a long time. Relationships don't come easily though. Trust, one of the main cords of healthy relationships, feels impossible because of the betrayal they experienced. Ironically, victims of sexual abuse long for close relationships as much as they fear them. They fear that allowing someone to become a caring friend will cause suppressed feelings to emerge.

Living like two people in one person, they put their game face on to survive "normal" life and fight off the feeling that there's nothing normal about their lives. Although vulnerability is necessary for gaining freedom, whom can they trust?

A dark secret that couldn't remain hidden (Sue's story)

My first encounter with a victim of sexual abuse was Sue. I was immediately impressed with her. She always seemed eager to learn, cheerful and friendly—a delight to have around. Everything about her made me think she must have had a healthy 18-year factor. Yet this outgoing university freshman carried a dark secret.

As time passed, Sue could no longer maintain the happy demeanor she wanted others to see. She began to turn to excessive behaviors of exercise, dieting, and sleeping. Battling feelings of depression and despair, she tried desperately to gain control of her life while feeling helplessly out of control.

The past devoured the present

What could have caused such a sudden and extreme change? There was a story behind her story, and it wasn't good. At the advice of a caring friend, she nervously called to request a meeting with me. In an act of tremendous courage, Sue allowed me to be the first person to hear the dark secret she had been carrying. During one dreadful visit to her grandparents' home when Sue was only twelve years old, her grandfather entered her room and sexually molested her.

Suffering silently, Sue tried to hide and suppress this unimaginable betrayal of trust and violation of her life. She finally reached a breaking point and could no longer sustain the self that she wanted to be. The past devoured the present, and her life began to fall apart.

Just get over it?

Imagine what it does to a little girl's sense of identity and security when her grandfather sexually violates her. How would Sue feel if someone told her to "just get over it" or "forgive him and move on"? How is she supposed to do this? Careless advice like this is both unrealistic and hurtful to the victims of deep betrayal and abuse. Naive counsel only makes victims feel more like a failure. Without loving intervention from a caring friend and guidance from a counselor, Sue would continue her struggle with crippling and destructive emotions that would lead to a broken trail of damaged relationships.

Sexual abuse and marriage

Before entering a marriage relationship, victims of sexual abuse should first address their pain. As mentioned before, a healthy marriage (or any close family relationship, for that matter) requires vulnerability, transparency, and trust. Because allowing for these qualities feels too risky, they are painfully difficult for victims of sexual abuse. On the other hand, marriage can provide a helpful context for recovery and renewal through the love and devotion of a spouse. Typically, however, a wise counselor is needed.

The person who marries a victim of sexual abuse is often surprised by the effects of the abuse. It's not uncommon for the mate of a victim to feel frustrated, confused and helpless. Making matters worse, they can often interpret the victim's behavior as a personal affront. When victims put up walls or shut down their emotions or push away from sexual intimacy, their mates interpret it as rejection or personal failure. The intimacy of marriage requires levels of vulnerability that survivors feel unable to give. Adult victims of child sexual abuse must seek wise counsel if they want to enjoy healthy, thriving relationships. If you observe the signs described in Sue's story, offer caring friendship to that person. We can help those who suffer in agonizing silence through sensitivity and caring friendship.

Confronting the perpetrator

Gaining freedom to move forward into a healthier future always requires confrontation of the perpetrator. If this cannot happen face to face or if it's unwise to confront the abuser in person, a letter or a form of role-playing are both adequate means of confrontation.

Confronting a perpetrator gives a victim the opportunity to regain a sense of control. It provides an outlet for verbally articulating raw emotions and pain in a way that places responsibility on the perpetrator. Though we cannot go back and change what happened, we can change ourselves. Likewise, the only thing we can change about the past is how we allow it to affect us in our future.

Sue did write a letter to her grandfather. He was on his deathbed at the time (which was shockingly used by a relative to inflict a sense of guilt on her). Her grandfather did write back, and his letter was one of the saddest things I've ever read. He begged for his granddaughter's forgiveness. Thankfully, this was a turning point for Sue. It empowered her to leverage her suffering to help many other people.

Victims of sexual abuse face many formidable obstacles on their path to freedom. Those who endured sexual abuse must remember that the evil actions of others victimized them. As hard as it might be, they must reject self-blame and the blame other people try to project onto them. They also need counteracting truths in their abuse memory file to use against the powerful emotions of shame, guilt, and fear.

Death of a parent or sibling

"I go down to the basement" (Mike's story)

Another significant disruption of the 18-year factor is the death of a parent or sibling. While in middle school, Mike endured the tragic loss of his older sister, a high school senior. She was honored for both athletics and academics and had a scholarship for a respected university. An automobile accident claimed her life shortly before her high school graduation. On that day, this young man lost his sister *and* his parents. His parents did not physically pass away, but they were so lost in their grief that they became unavailable to this young man.

Years later, I asked him how he survived such a traumatic family loss. He recalled, "I just went to the basement and played video games." I then asked if he still goes down to the basement when life is difficult. After thinking for a moment, with a startled look on his face, he answered, "Yes, as a matter of fact, I still go to the basement." He didn't recognize how this survival mechanism carried over into his adult life.

Sometimes severe dysfunctions follow as a result of significant disruptions. Below, John tells the backstory to his life—a story spanning four generations. His story, a self-described "twisted history of pain, confusion and anger," is a powerful reminder of how one person's choices can send disruptive effects to future generations.

"My great-grandfather affected four generations"
(John's story)

The actions of my great-grandfather, George, had a lasting impact on my family. When he was young and unmarried, he was involved with two women, one of whom became pregnant. Just before giving birth to the child who would be my grandfather, they got married. But about two years later, when they were expecting another child, they made a decision that would shape the future in ways that hurt many people. To hide the shame of their first child conceived out of wedlock, they sent him (my grandfather) away to live with his grandparents.

While living away from his parents, my grandfather never received a birthday card or Christmas card, let alone an invitation to return home. Although he had six siblings, only one brother and one sister made any effort to have a relationship with him. Years later, when he got married, he and his wife had two boys, one of whom is my father.

In a strange twist of irony, my great-grandparents ended up raising their grandson when their daughter conceived and gave birth out of wedlock. Yet my grandfather (their son born out of wedlock) and his "promiscuous sister" were left out of the will.

I can't imagine what my grandfather felt from being abandoned by his parents. Although he tried not to be controlled by resentment, his deep hurt and anger led to a hard-nosed and controlling approach to his own family. My father then imitated my grandfather's behavior (although to a diminished extent), and I also carried the behavior patterns with me. When I met the woman who became my wife, behavior patterns from my family history became a challenge to our relationship. After I got counsel, I began to overcome the generational effects of my great-grandfather's actions.

My father told me of a time when he was driving with my grandpa through the countryside, and grandpa (in his late 70's) unexpectedly broke down in tears because he was still agonizing over the pain of rejection and unanswered questions about why his parents abandoned him.

A victim of human trafficking (Joe's story)

Joe's story reveals how severe dysfunction in the home could cause significant disruption—one that changed the course of his life for many years. His father favored him above his siblings in their large family. The obvious disproportionate love his father showed him turned Joe into the object of sibling envy and hatred. Because of envy, his brothers never spoke kindly to him. A powerful and destructive force, envy hates its object and looks to eliminate it.

Unimaginably, when Joe was seventeen, they secretly sold him to a group of men to be a slave. For the next seventeen years of Joe's life, he was tossed from one master to another, while his father assumed he had been killed and abandoned the search. What would that traumatic experience do to a young man as he spends the "best years of his life" held captive?

We must be honest about painful childhood experiences that cause a notable disruption to our 18-year factor. Along with significant disruptions, serious dysfunctions during our upbringing deserve close consideration as well. We will explore these more fully in the next chapter.

Chapter 6: Evaluation and Discussion

1. Was there an event or experience in your 18-year factor that caused a significant disruption? Can you see ways that it continues to influence your life? Explain.

2. What is your response to the myths about the effects of divorce on children?

3. What is your response to the truths about sexual abuse?

4. What did you learn or connect with from the stories of Sue, Mike, John, and Joe?

Chapter 7

Severe dysfunctions

Perhaps you grew up under a father with an unpredictable temper or a father who was aloof and distant. Maybe it was a mother who always seemed to be in a bad mood or always responded negatively to you. Some recall a perfectionist parent who made everyone feel as if they never did things the right way. Others remember excessively controlling parents or a parent who consistently used manipulative communication. Many say their parents were always fighting. These are examples of severe dysfunction.

Dysfunction can range from seemingly harmless to very damaging. A severe dysfunction is a pervasive characteristic in a home that makes it an unhealthy and harmful place. It's something (or someone) that makes the air toxic. A severe dysfunction actively and passively forces others to adjust to unhealthy interpersonal behaviors, expectations, and interactions.

Severe dysfunctions cause lasting effects on children. A woman in her mid-sixties told me that she still feels the shadow of her perfectionist mother over her shoulders when she cleans her home. "Not a crumb on the table" she recalled. If you grew up in a home that had a severe dysfunction, it would likely cause significant challenges to your adult relationships.

Dysfunctional parents are the most common source of trouble for children. When a child is forced to adapt to adult immaturity or subject to adult abuses, it sends lasting effects into his adult life. When I observe extreme reactions and imbalanced impulses in adults, I usually assume that there's a story behind them that traces back to childhood experiences.

Let's take a closer look at some of the more common and life-altering dysfunctions. We'll consider addictions, disorders, and abuses (physical and verbal).

Alcohol, drugs and other addictions

A severe dysfunction that many children experience is living in a home where one or both parents are addicted to drugs or alcohol. My mother grew up with an alcoholic father (my grandfather), and she once told me that she never had a meaningful conversation with her father during her upbringing. She does, however, recall many nights of helping her mom clean up her dad to get him to bed. My grandfather was what people identify as a "functional alcoholic."

When an alcoholic downplays his addiction by saying, "At least I am providing for my family," he exposes his self-deception. While it's true that non-functional alcoholic parents wreak more havoc in the lives of children, this truth should never be used to minimize the damage done by men like my grandfather.

Other addictions like gambling, pornography, or even a father's time-consuming attachment to video games bring dysfunction to families. Looking back at your upbringing and identifying lasting effects is essential if you had a parent who battled an addiction.

Disorders

As with addictions, we should look closely at the effects on our lives if our parents battled life-altering disorders. While obsessive and controlling behaviors resulting from personality disorders can create a habitat for dysfunction, I'd like to focus on two of the most common disorders: depressive and anxiety.

Depressive disorder

A depressive disorder is perhaps the most common one affecting both parents and children. Outpatient treatment of depression increased 300% by the end of the 20th century.[1] Antidepressant medications are the most significant selling prescription drugs in America.[2] Depressive disorder can be debilitating in ways that make life difficult for everyone.

We find a variety of traits in a depressive disorder. It could appear in a depressed mood and diminished interest or pleasure in activities. The person might experience an intense feeling of sadness that takes the energy and value out of life—a demotivating feeling that paralyzes the person, accompanied by feelings of indecisiveness, worthlessness, and sometimes excessive guilt. Oftentimes, it affects a person's ability to concentrate and changes his/her sleep patterns. A parent with depressive disorder profoundly affects the home-life of children in ways that go with them well into adulthood, often causing significant stress on relationships in their adult life.

Anxiety disorder

When a parent has an anxiety disorder, excessive fears repeatedly disrupt or disable family life. Children in these homes have to adjust to the parents in ways that leave lasting effects on them. These parents tend to issue excessive warnings about realistic and unrealistic dangers. Consequently, they overly shield their children from the normal activities and experiences of childhood. When parents talk without restraint about their anxieties, children will likely internalize what they hear in unhealthy ways.

Parental anxiety disorder often causes children to become adults who battle unnecessary fears and inhibitions, not reaching their potential because of worries over perceived risks. Anxious parents tend to order life around predictable rather than spontaneous and adventurous experiences. Their fear-based restrictions are more about their own need to feel better than what is best for their children. Excessive control is a "traveling companion" of anxiety, and as they work cooperatively, they can make a home feel more like a prison. These parents sometimes unnecessarily incite rebellion in children who want to escape the prison.

Physical, mental, and verbal abuse

Physical, mental, and verbal abuse are equally severe

dysfunctions that exert destructive effects on children. These forms of abuse stem from immature, self-centered parents who are easily irritated and quickly angered. As a result, family-life becomes toxic and unsafe for children. Jill's story illustrates the effects of growing up in a home with daily experiences of anger, violence, and abuse.

A life trapped in violence (Jill's story)

I grew up in a home where conflict, rage, and abuse were everyday occurrences. I never understood why this was happening to me, but I knew something was wrong with our home. I heard other children talk, and it appeared that they had ordinary families. I longed for love and attention, but I kept my feelings bottled up because I didn't know where to put them. Much of my childhood was spent crying, and I was often fearful that my mother would kill me. My mother once told me that she wished she had gotten rid of my siblings and me when she had the chance. My heart would break every time she said something like that. I lived in this trap of violence for seventeen years until I finally fled. I turned to male companionship and became involved in sexual relationships in the hope that I would find someone who would love and care for me. I did not even care if drugs were involved as long as we were having fun and I could cling to the hope of a lasting relationship that was free from violence. Eventually, I found myself married to a man who was extremely controlling and had a violent temper. I was back in a terrorizing situation. It didn't take long for me to run from that situation. I was in the habit of running from situations that I could not control. But leaving my marriage only brought another devastating blow to my self-esteem.

I did not know how to handle pressure of any kind until I was well into my forties. I often wondered what my life would have been like if I had grown up in a "normal" home. What else could I have accomplished if my confidence in my abilities had not been challenged at such a young age and to such a degree?

I will never know. All I can do is understand that when I was young, instead of being nurtured in times when normally a lesson could have been learned, I was beaten and subjected to words of hatred. This created emotions and feelings that I was unable to understand. I went out into a big world unprepared for the realities that exist in everyday living. Like so many others, I escaped into the world of gambling, drugs, and alcohol --still trying to run from the terrors of abuse I experienced as a young child.

It was when I realized that what happened to me as a child was not my fault that my life began to change. When I realized that I am a loveable person, my life began to take on new meaning. I was finally able to forgive my mother for the atrocities she inflicted upon me as a child.

Jill was attached to her past under buried feelings and fears, with self-blame being the most potent. As mentioned earlier, children tend to misread what happens *to* them as an indication of something wrong *with* them. Imagine a little girl thinking that she deserved or caused her parent's abusive anger and violence. This way of thinking is a common attachment to a painful past.

It helps to know that what you experienced as a child was not your fault. Carrying the fears that you felt as a child is bondage. These buried feelings and fears can only be uncovered and resolved by looking back and facing them. Close examination can help you connect attitudes and behaviors with the baggage of your childhood.

Verbal abuse

Most everyone knows the children's rhyme, "Sticks and stones may break my bones, but words shall never hurt me." Contrary to the message of the rhyme, those who endured verbal abuse as children know the power of words. Because the damage of verbal abuse is more subtle than physical abuse, some well-intentioned people minimize the effects of verbal abuse by saying, "At least your parents didn't beat you." As we saw in the chapter two stories of Jerry ("Dummy") and Nora, children are often unaware of the damaging ways that verbal abuse shapes their lives. Aileen put it this way:

> I didn't know that the way my mother talked to me wasn't the way other mothers talked to their daughters. I was an only child, and her constant criticism and putting me down made me feel terrible about myself, and it made me double my efforts to please her. More than anything, I wanted my mother to be happy with me. I was probably 30 before I realized there was nothing normal about how she talked to me. Not that the recognition helped because I still wanted her to be happy with me. At 50, I'm still trying to recover.[3]

Unfortunately, verbal abuse is often passed down through generations. It is not long before young parents catch themselves saying, "I sound so much like my father or mother." Even tones of voice are important. What are the possible long-term effects of the following tones?

Belittling
Critical
Minimizing
Mocking
Condescending
Bossy
Angry
Snobby
Frustrated
Defensive
Moody
Distant
Disrespectful
Dark
Whining

In contrast, verbal affirmation and encouragement (along with proper tones of expression) are equally capable of making long-lasting beneficial effects.

After the movie "Kramer vs. Kramer" was released in 1979, Michelle recalls asking her mom if there was a custody battle over her and hearing a disheartening "no."

"Your dad didn't want you" (Michelle's story)

My mom was a divorcee when she met the young man who would be my dad, and my impending arrival led them to the altar. I have very few memories from my childhood years with them because they divorced when I was five. On one very memorable day preceding the divorce, however, I vividly recall a physical fight between them, during which my mom told me to run to the neighbor and call the police. I ran but my dad ran after me and brought me back. I can't recall the words between them during this fight, but I remember riding in the car next to my mom and seeing her broken eyeglasses. I also remember her tears. Within a year or so, I recall riding in a car with my dad as he told me he was leaving the East Coast and moving to Colorado. Through my cries and tears, I begged him to stay. He left.

When I was seven, my mom married my stepfather. Years later, my dad returned to our hometown. The three of them tried to establish a "normal" relationship, where my dad would have me on some weekends. Truthfully, they did the best they could. My friends were amazed that my three parents were so amicable! I spent most of my growing up years with my mom and stepfather, and as long as I appeared to be the perfect daughter, I earned my stepfather's approval.

I did not seek my stepfather's affection; in hindsight, I think I subconsciously viewed that as a betrayal of my dad. In my stepfather's weekly subscription to a pornographic magazine, I repeatedly saw images and read stories that gave me a warped perception of women and their role in male-female relationships. The fact that he enjoyed this magazine gave me a distaste for any physical contact with him, so we had an agreeable relationship without any meaningful father-daughter affection. My mom, on the other hand, tried to love me enough for both of them. I know she regretted not wanting me at the conception of life.

When I left for college, all of my parental restraints and accountability were gone, and my hunger for male affection and affirmation found a smorgasbord of opportunity. To coin the overused cliché, I went "looking for love in all the wrong places." Though I didn't understand it at the time, my pursuit of male approval converged with a desire to gain a feeling of control over my life. No one was going to hurt me by leaving me because I would do the leaving. As soon as I gained affection and intimacy from a guy, I was off to the next one. I also didn't fully understand how I used alcohol to escape bad feelings about myself for being so promiscuous. I was empty and broken but I didn't realize it. The fun and pleasure masked my inner feelings. The fact that "everyone was doing it" justified my choices.

After college, I met the man who would be my husband. On our first date, he showed me home movies from his childhood, and I was sold! Here was a man who had an idyllic childhood! I saw him as a man who would make a perfect father to my children and that's what I wanted more than anything—a good father. I pursued him and won. It wasn't until later that I learned from his sister that their childhood was not as idyllic as I thought. In the video images from his childhood, his father appeared nurturing and charming. Absent from the videos was his father's dysfunctional behavior and his longtime mistress.

My husband-to-be recognized what he called "my domineering personality," and yet he still asked me to be his wife. I was in control and he was (strangely) happy to allow me to be. After our first of two children arrived, I began to realize that something was missing within me. I think I started to assess my life, my sense of morality, my feelings of brokenness. I understood that I didn't want my children to do the things I did, but I had no idea how to form a standard of morality and how to teach it to children. I also didn't understand what it meant to have a healthy marriage.

My stepfather had committed adultery for years while I was in high school and college and finally put my mom through a very painful and debilitating divorce. At the same time, (as we were expecting our second child) I wondered if my husband would struggle with adultery and repeat the habits he learned from his father.

In my journey to healing, I came to understand that my parents began their own lives with broken childhoods. My mother had an alcoholic father who took her along to bars and struggled even to speak the words "I love you" to his dying day. My father recently told me that his parents never told him they loved him or expressed approval. My stepfather was tossed from foster home to foster home, as his mother and father did not want him. They played the game of life with the hands they were dealt.

Physical and emotional neglect

Some severe dysfunctions involve passive forms of abuse. Parents who deprive their children of consistent, loving discipline and mature guidance send them into adult life unprepared for its challenges and temptations. Various forms of parental deprivation often supply the story behind adult feelings of insecurity and vulnerability.

Consider Julie's story about the effects of parental deprivation. Her story reveals how parents deprive children in ways that stay with them in adult life.

Hurt by a distant father (Julie's story)

Julie learned from her father that love had to be earned. Good behavior merited her father's favor, whereas disobedience to his standards and beliefs drew his anger and distance. It was all about performance. She received approval from her dad if she displayed to others what he thought to be right and proper behavior. As long as she pretended to be the obedient and respectful child, she was accepted. She grew up not really knowing her father's love but trying desperately to gain it. He was absent emotionally and, as a grown woman, Julie does not know him, though she still clearly hears his disapproval.

As Julie grew up, she made more choices that displeased her dad. According to him, she did not eat, dress, or date appropriately. Rather than gaining what her heart desired, she was farther away from the hope of ever being loved for who she was. As a result, she turned to other male relationships to find affirmation and acceptance. During this phase of her life, the connection with her father severed completely.

Julie became a people-pleasing, empty, broken mess. All her male relationships only further splintered her soul. When she could not bear the self-deception any longer, she enrolled in a Bible College as a final effort to ease the overwhelming pain in her heart. Perhaps total abandonment to God would release her from consuming turmoil and grant her the acceptance from her father. If she embraced God, she thought that perhaps the emptiness of her heart would fade away.

During her time at college, Julie began to see layers of deception to her troubled mind and determined to be honest about herself and to seek God's plan for her life. When she finally stopped running, she met a stable guy and married him, believing her past could now become a distant memory.

Distant, but not forgotten...

For the next seventeen years of marriage, Julie was baffled by unexplainable outbursts of anger and an almost continual feeling of discontentment—even though she was married to a loving, supportive husband and had four beautiful children. What could be missing?

Unable to pinpoint the cause of her unrest, she finally broke. Julie hit a wall and admitted failure—personal, marital, parental, social and to her dismay, even spiritual. Attacked on all fronts, everything she tried so hard to keep in balance came simultaneously crashing down. Depression consumed her for the next three years. More from Julie's story later...

The most deceptive kinds of attachments to the past are the protective mechanisms children use to survive a difficult upbringing. The role of protective mechanisms during the 18-year factor is the next point of evaluation.

Chapter 7: Evaluation and Discussion

1. Do you recall a severe dysfunction from your 18-year factor? Please explain.

2. How did any of the opening examples of dysfunction connect with your experience?

3. Can you identify in your life any extreme reactions or imbalanced impulses that trace back to your upbringing?

4. Did you grow up under a parent or guardian who battled addictions or disorders?

5. Did you experience physical or verbal abuse as a child? Explain.

6. Did you experience physical or emotional neglect as a child? Explain.

7. What did you learn or connect with from the stories of Jill, Michelle, and Julie?

Chapter 8

Unsafe protective mechanisms

Which word doesn't belong to the title, "Post-traumatic stress disorder"? Answer: "Disorder."

There is nothing "disordered" about post-traumatic stress after experiencing the traumatic realities of war. The mind and body respond in normal and expected (ordered) ways of self-protection after enduring trauma. Labeling this as a "disorder" is not helpful to those who struggle to overcome the *ordered* responses to the trauma of war. Of course, there is perhaps an element of "disorder" when it feels difficult to live in normal (civilian) life after the effects of traumatic stress. The challenge they face is gradually separating the thoughts, emotions, and physical reactions caused by the trauma from circumstances and experiences post-trauma.

Children also deal with a kind of post-traumatic stress after being traumatized throughout their 18-year factor. Although we couldn't really label their experience as "post-adverse childhood disorder," they also face a similar challenge of gradually separating the thoughts, emotions, and physical reactions caused by the trauma from circumstances and experiences post-trauma. If they do not understand and find freedom from the self-protective responses used to survive a troubled upbringing, they will not be able to enjoy healthy adult relationships.

We never talked to each other about it (Brenda's story)

Growing up in a severely traumatized home, Brenda spoke of a powerful protective mechanism used to survive the abuses of her alcoholic father. When her father was in a drunken condition, he would often line the children up on a couch and make their mother sit in a chair in front of them. He would then hold a shotgun to their mother's head and threaten to shoot her as he called her a dirty cheating whore.

Predictably, these traumatized children would beg their daddy not to kill their mommy. This scene repeatedly played out during her childhood. Along with other horrible effects from this abuse, Brenda (now in her sixties) recalled something unexpected. "Strange as it might seem, as siblings we never talked with each other about these things." When asked why she thought they didn't talk about it, she answered, "I guess we thought it would become real if we talked about it."

What did she mean "become real"? Did these children suppress the horrifying reality of their father's abuse by not talking about it? Actually, their response is not at all strange. Just as many who endure the trauma of wartime are unwilling to talk about their experiences, children in severely dysfunctional homes often choose not to talk about their experiences. Suppression and denial play both a protective as well as a harmful role during and after trauma. When actual reality is too painful to accept, unreality becomes a preferred state of mind. Sadly, a child's learned instinct to shift from reality to unreality becomes an adult's unhealthy avoidance mechanism that hurts his or her adult relationships.

Protective mechanisms

Protective mechanisms develop when children are forced to find ways to survive adverse effects of adult behavior. Children instinctively turn to these mechanisms but do not necessarily consciously choose them; rather, they develop them as a means of adaptation for living under the effects of abusive adult behavior.

The most common protective mechanisms include shutting down, putting up walls, walking away or hiding from conflict, defensively overreacting, overcompensating for bad experiences, and shifting to imaginary realities. All of these serve their protective purposes. Yet it's difficult to help people see how their childhood protective mechanisms are affecting their adult lives. Suppression of painful memories blurs an ability to see connections between the past and the present. Consider the story behind the story from a college friend of mine.

When I pretended to sleep, he wouldn't beat me
(Stewart's story)

What is it like for a child to listen for the footsteps of a drunken father with fear that he will come into his bedroom to physically or mentally abuse him? Far too many children live with this fear.

During my college years, Stewart needed a place to live to escape the abuse of his stepfather. His stepdad had a violent temper and physically abused him and his mother for years. When he lay in his bed listening to his stepfather beat his mother, he did his best to pretend he was sleeping. He told me that his stepdad would never hurt him if he thought he was asleep.

When my friend told me this part of his painful story, I immediately made a connection that he never saw. He would always go to bed at strange times while living at our house. We came to understand that whenever life became stressful, he would simply go to bed. He didn't realize how his protective mechanism from his childhood experience carried over into his young adult life.

Exploding and withdrawing

Protective mechanisms often involve dramatic overreactions and protective under-reactions. When children are forced to deal with circumstances far beyond their maturity level, they typically don't know how to verbalize their frustrations and feelings. It's not uncommon for them to respond with dramatic overreactions like nagging, harassing, or screaming. Other children turn to protective under-reactions like withdrawing by avoiding, sulking and silence.

Children rarely leave these responses behind when they enter adulthood. A protective mechanism that plays a role for a long-time during childhood years will likely continue in adult life and relationships. When children felt hurt, misunderstood or neglected, they commonly react as adults by exploding and withdrawing. These protective mechanisms of isolation and insulation make adult relationships complicated and confusing.

Unfortunately, adults who carry these mechanisms into relationships are often unaware of why they react as they do. Suppression and denial play a significant role in blinding adults to the lingering effects of their childhood reactions. Dominant reactions, however, rarely come without a history. Adults need to understand the story behind their story. They need to know why they turn to dramatic overreactions or retreat to harmful under-reactions. Ultimately, they need to recognize how protective mechanisms *bind them* to a painful past and *blind them* to the damage caused in adult relationships.

Attached to the past by fear and control

Significantly disrupted and severely dysfunctional homes are unsafe and unstable places that make children feel insecure or afraid. It's not uncommon for those with a painful past to use the protective mechanism of control to minimize the fears in their troubled upbringing. These children often become adults who continue to try to control life and people to afford them a feeling of safety and security—to keep fear at bay.

Fear and control function as a kind of glue that cements past and present with a strong potential of ruining the future. Fear of what happened in the past ignites unnecessary and excessive efforts to control the present. In her story of life in a severely dysfunctional home with a verbally abusive mother, Jill acknowledged that it caused her to form a "habit of running from situations that I could not control."

Like most protective mechanisms, living out of fear and control especially hurts adult relationships. Fear of damage caused by someone from the past becomes redirected at someone in the present, who is then placed (unfairly) under control lest he or she do similar things. The use of control becomes a payment that person must pay for the pain caused by others. The tendency to control other adults conveys distrust and disrupts otherwise positive relationships. It also exposes an unhealthy attachment to a painful past. Fear and control destroy the possibility of true love because love flourishes only in a relationship of trust and freedom.

Contractual relationships

A person who allows fear and control to dominate his life places unnecessary and suffocating demands on others. Those who are held hostage by fear of the past approach relationships with self-serving expectations. They fight off fear by approaching relationships on a kind of contractual arrangement. "I need you to_____. I expect you to_____. I demand you to_____. If you fail, I will punish you by exploding or withdrawing."

A mate dealing with fear and control in a spouse often finds himself saying:

"I am not your father," or "I am not your mother."

"Please stop projecting onto me what they did to you."

"I understand that your father rejected you, but I won't reject you."

"You don't need to hedge around me, I won't lash out the way your father did."

A couple can build a healthier future free from bondage to the past when the dynamics of fear and control are understood and responded to with patience and mercy.

Highly protective and suspicious

Adverse childhood experiences give children a feeling of instability, insecurity, and fear. Life feels unpredictable and unsafe. Some children who experience high exposure to adversity turn to high-risk behaviors that make them highly susceptible to health and relationship difficulties. Many of these behaviors (alcohol and drug use, gambling, unrestrained sexual involvement, workaholism, etc.) are means of escape from the pain of the past.

Other traumatized children withdraw into a protective and suspicious disposition because the risks of vulnerability, transparency, and trust are too frightening. Highly protective and suspicious adults should look back to ask if there is a story behind their approach to life and to people.

Large-scale generalizations

Painful childhood experiences (and the protective mechanisms used to survive them) tend to cause children to adopt irrational large-scale generalizations about all of life and all people. Although their suffering occurs in a specific context involving a small number of people, the magnitude of the pain at this vulnerable time of life is more significant than most understand. Specific adverse childhood experiences form a template that shapes a child's expectations of other people and circumstances. A young girl's withdrawn or violent father leads her to believe that all men are like him. Her mother's resentment toward her father further supports a large-scale generalization about "all" men. Though such generalizations are irrational, we can understand how the rational part of life was damaged by past experiences.

Consider the story of a mother whose negative influence controlled her daughter's thinking and habits well past childhood years.

I get out of the car quickly (Cindy's story)

Cindy had to overcome the effects of her mother's extreme resentment toward her father before she could trust a man enough to marry him. Cindy's parents divorced when she was about twelve years old. Though her father was not a good man, her mother's bitterness toward him profoundly shaped Cindy's heart regarding *all* men. When Cindy and her siblings spent weekends with their father, her mother programmed them, even *required them*, to send a nonverbal message to him by getting out of his car quickly when he dropped them off.

When Cindy was twenty-five years old, she met Bill, a good man who became her husband five years later. It took Bill five years of patient love to overcome Cindy's damaged view of men. Bill recounted to me that when he and Cindy were first dating, he had to ask her to allow him to stop his car completely before she got out of it. At twenty-five years of age, Cindy was unaware of how and why she got out of the car quickly. Bill simply understood her action as unsafe. He didn't know the history behind it until later. It's hard to imagine a parent using her children as tools for expressing her bitterness, but it happens more often than most realize. Parents must understand the power they have to set templates for their children—damaging templates that usually stay with them for years.

Two people in one person

Many adults who had a painful upbringing tell me that they feel they live between two identities. They see it as a matter of survival. Although they put their game face on to survive the real world, they feel growing stress over hiding their other side. Sometimes it feels unbearable to maintain the act. They speak of fear that their duplicity will be exposed and others will discover their darker side. Their battle between two identities also makes them distrustful of the genuineness of others. They believe that every Jekyll has his Hyde, whom he cannot control and who threatens to take him over.

The "two identity challenge" often traces back to the way children in a dysfunctional home learn to change to gain the love and acceptance of their parents or guardians. Trying to be the kind of child their parents will love, they fear that letting down their mask will risk losing that love. This learned habit often involves creating a false self—the one they present to others for approval. Finding their true identity is not easy because it feels unsafe.

Consider Abigail, a woman who confessed that she lived with an addiction that lasted over thirty years.

An unhealthy approval addiction (Abigail's story)

My story is one full of regrets, hurts, and being unlovable. Strangely, it began in a home that seemed much like a fairy tale. I grew up in a loving and caring home, never lacking anything. I lived with a mother and a father who loved each other and provided for their children. I was a happy child who enjoyed life. Later, however, I realized that I adopted many insecurities and wrong mindsets during my upbringing that I had to break away from and learn how to conquer. I especially had to overcome childhood fears. Being rejected and imperfect is my ultimate fear. I grew up with an unhealthy and unrealistic belief that I needed to be flawless to be loved.

I did not want to disappoint others, so I created a false image of myself. I would try to impress others by becoming just like them to feel accepted. If people were disappointed in me or did not like me, I would be distraught and try to win them over by doing anything to get their approval, even if it meant going against my values.

I created an unhealthy approval addiction that lasted over thirty years. I cannot say I have fully overcome these insecurities, but I have boundaries in place to protect myself.

How I overcame these fears was not a simple task. I had to go back into my past hurts and failures to see the root of the problem. I had to relive moments that I was not proud of and work through the emotions. As I was trying to find peace from my past, it brought on more guilt and shame into my life. Through trying to process these hurts and failures, I became depressed. I hurt my family with harsh words. I lost friendships due to isolation, and I missed big events in my family's life due to depression.

I was haunted daily by the fear of rejection and loneliness. The fear became a reality, and I created a life filled with negative mindsets and false accusations. I thought everyone was against me, and I had to protect myself from being hurt. I tried to look normal on the outside when everything within me was chaotic. During this time, I broke off an engagement, stopped communicating with my family for almost a year, lost my best friend and roommate, almost lost my job, and left my church due to feeling judged.

Life was falling apart, and I did not know where to go for help. In the midst of all this chaos, the doctor put me on antidepressants and a strong sleeping pill. The prescribed medicine put me into a more profound depression. I could think clearly but did not know what to do with my thoughts. I felt like a zombie with no control over my emotions. I became an angry person, not caring what others thought about me.

One night I was tired of hurting those around me by my actions and words and did not want to live another day. I was miserable and afraid. This was not the first time to think these thoughts, but it was the first time that I wanted to act on them.

Tears are rolling down my face as I am writing my story. I know that this was a low moment in my life. I still struggle with the fact that I wanted to end my life. I picked up my prescription sleeping pills off the bedside table and thought about taking just enough so I would not wake up in the morning to another dreadful day. No one was at my home to stop me. Not many people I associated with knew I was depressed because I kept my thoughts to myself. No one would have guessed that I had suicidal thoughts.

Instead of taking the pills, I fell asleep with the pill bottle in my hand. I woke up the next morning with the bottle next to me on my bed, never opened. Since that day, I have fought for purpose in my life and asked God back into my heart. It has taken me nearly seven years to heal the hurt and shame from these events.

It was difficult to write my story because I was fearful of being rejected or looked at differently because of my past. Writing my story, however, helped me turn my past hurts and failures into something useful to help others. I have been too fearful to speak out, but now I am learning what it means to be transparent. I am learning how to trust God with my story completely. Perhaps you can benefit from what I experienced and turn your story into something that can help others.

Why do protective mechanisms become unsafe?

The lifespan of a protective mechanism extends well beyond the original childhood circumstances. The longer children live with a protective mechanism, the more deeply it becomes part of their nature. When something or someone triggers a reminder of the original pain, these mechanisms form a kind of default setting that causes an adult to irrationally and unnecessarily project the past onto the present. Protective mechanisms from childhood commonly become overreactions in adulthood. This tendency is particularly harmful to relationships.

How protective mechanisms affect relationships

A single adult can live relatively undisturbed with her childhood mechanisms in place. The trouble begins when she desires close and intimate relationships with other adults. Why are these mechanisms are harmful to intimate relationships? Because protective mechanisms undermine three essentials to close friendship and especially marriage.

Vulnerability, transparency, and trust?

Meaningful and healthy friendships and solid marriages require the qualities of vulnerability, transparency, and trust. Protective mechanisms work against these qualities. Why? Because protective mechanisms are instinctive (not necessarily conscious) risk-reducing defaults for children who are forced to survive dysfunctional homes. Fear and distrust become a way of life for children who are hurt by those who should have been the safest and most trusted people in their lives.

A wife who lived with constant conflict during her upbringing found that it was safest to shut down during a dispute. When disagreements arise with her husband, she shuts down. Her husband, unfortunately, thinks that he did something wrong. When he inquires as to why his wife shuts down during a disagreement, she might become defensive about him asking. She (unknowingly) reacts to his question as an attack against the protective mechanism that helped her survive her painful past. She responds this way without clearly understanding what she is doing and why she is doing it.

Adults who survived toxic upbringings give extended life to the damage caused by them when they cling to protective mechanisms. They sabotage their relationships in seemingly irrational and confusing ways. I've witnessed far too many examples of a painful past becoming the thief of future intimacy. Thriving marriages require levels of vulnerability, transparency, and trust that feel inaccessible to those who shielded themselves from adults for many years. They prefer the safety of protectively circling the wagons to reduce the risk of more hurt—even though it hurts those who would never hurt them.

Removing protective mechanisms

Something unsettling often occurs when someone begins to drop a protective guard and become transparent and vulnerable. Significant unmet needs lie under the surface of a protective shield. When someone is honest about the lingering effects of a troubled upbringing, cravings for things children need from loving adults awaken.

These important unmet needs can lead to unrealistic expectations of those who are close to a person trying to overcome the past. It might show up in excessive need for affirmation, acceptance, and security due to years of feeling worthless, unnecessary, and insecure.

Relationship challenges

Healthy adult relationships are essential to a path for a better future. A caring friend or mate, however, will feel suffocated and inadequate if he is expected to satisfy unmet needs from a painful childhood. Those who are trying to overcome a painful past must be aware of the danger of pushing caring people away by expecting more from them than they're capable of giving. A husband should not be expected to take the place of a wife's dysfunctional father; a man cannot be husband and father at the same time. On the other hand, a husband can rebuild a woman's confidence in men damaged by her father.

Understanding the reality of unmet needs can protect someone struggling to overcome the past from siphoning the life out of caring, healthy people, and from suffocating good relationships. Caring friends must remind themselves that unmet needs exist because of abusive acts of parental mistreatment and neglect. Consequently, wisely guarded and guided expectations are essential.

Chapter 8: Evaluation and Discussion

1. What does the author believe to be wrong with the label "Post-traumatic stress disorder"?
2. How do severely troubled homes affect a child's approach to reality?
3. What are protective mechanisms and how do they develop?
4. What are some examples of protective mechanisms?
5. Have you ever struggled with protective mechanisms? (If yes, explain)
6. Why do adults fail to recognize protective mechanisms from their past?
7. What are dramatic overreactions and protective under reactions?
8. How do fear and control relate to the past, present, and future?
9. Can you identify ways that fear and control affect your life and relationships?
10. Summarize the author's concern about being highly protective and suspicious?
11. What are large-scale generalizations? Can you identify any in your life?
12. Have you experienced or observed the protective mechanism of living between two identities?
13. How do protective mechanisms affect adult relationships?
14. Summarize the warning for those who are struggling to overcome a painful past.

Chapter 9

Four kinds of children

Why do siblings respond differently to a dysfunctional home?

While dysfunctional homes cause many similar effects for children, not all respond/react the same way to those effects. My experience has led me to identify four main kinds of reactions to dysfunctional homes. Although children from a troubled upbringing will likely identify with elements from each, it's not uncommon for them to display one in a more emphasized way. Differences in a child's personality and temperament usually play a role in shaping his or her reaction to a painful upbringing.

Let me introduce you to the four kinds of children in relation to differences in reaction. The additional description (or nickname) in brackets would be from the dysfunctional parent's perspective.

1. The angry rebel (aka "our black sheep")
2. The peacemaking mediator (aka "our good girl")
3. The fleeing perfectionist (aka "our trophy")
4. The depressed defeatist (aka "our emotional one")

Let's delve further into these four reactions and consider the potential long-term effects of each.

1. The Angry Rebel (aka "our black sheep")

The angry rebel says, "I can't wait to get out of this place!" "I hate living here!" "These people are stupid!" Dysfunctional parents often label this child the "black sheep" of the family. Anger, of course, is a common emotion that boys in particular display when transitioning from adolescence to adulthood. During this time of life, hormonal and developmental changes incite a variety of emotions, which we've already noted in chapter five. In the case of the angry rebel, however, there's a clear connection between his anger, sadly misread as willful rebellion, and his dysfunctional home. He lacks the maturity to process circumstances created by his dysfunctional parent(s).

Strangely enough, the child labeled "angry rebel" might be the most honest one in the family. He might also be more accessible to help because anger is an emotion that connects more honestly with reality. Anger seems like a normal response when a child feels injured by those who should protect and care for him. Anger is not a form of suppression and denial.

Other children feel anger but suppress it to deny the painful reality of their troubled homes. They turn to various types of denial to escape rather than confront reality. Anger does not escape; it confronts. Adults who counsel these children are wise to recognize and connect with the elements of honesty in anger before helping the angry rebel to see the potential dangers in his anger.

"Anger" is one letter short of the word "danger," and the risks are indeed high for the angry rebel. Anger's destructive cousins—those that belong and easily expand within the same emotional family—include resentment, hatred, bitterness, and rage. When these emotions find a home in a person's heart, they make it toxic and put him at risk of dangerous behaviors. These emotions always destroy the container that carries them. Nothing good grows in a hate-filled heart.

Anger, resentment, hatred, and bitterness are difficult to dislodge from the heart because the person who feels them typically believes they are justified responses to the actions of others. This belief is then compounded by a victim mentality which makes the angry person feel free from responsibility for his emotions and actions. A victim mentality often leads to self-justified actions of retaliation.

Though all children feel the emotion of anger, parents are responsible for teaching them how to process it in healthy rather than destructive ways. Unfortunately, children in severely dysfunctional homes are not only deprived of this instruction, but those who should be their teachers are also the causes behind their anger. These children live under parents who stoke and feed anger and resentment.

No one should be surprised when the anger developed in childhood (and stoked by immature parents) leads to disproportionate overreactions redirected at undeserving objects. Anger looks for an outlet of expression. Children from dysfunctional homes commonly suppress anger at home in fear of an abusive parent and then release and redirect it at school or in other places. On the contrary, children who feel that home is a safe place generally open the release valve at home that they've kept tightly sealed at school, and this is healthy and preferable. I encourage parents to allow for some release at home where it can receive guidance.

Other children in dysfunctional homes might not outwardly express their anger, but we must not assume that they don't feel it. Differences in personality and temperament influence the ways children process anger. In my parenting, I told my children that life always involves anger-producing circumstances and anger-provoking people. Anger offers an opportunity for deciding what or who will control your life.

Anger can potentially turn control of our lives over to others, establishing a bond between a perpetrator and our hearts, which allows for more damage. It invites the neglectful and hurtful parent to take a seat in the control room of our hearts. If he hopes for freedom from the pain of the past, the angry rebel must understand this reality. He must ask himself if he desires to empower those who hurt him. Does he have the courage to leave home completely, or will he remain home emotionally after he leaves? Ninety percent of all relationship difficulties involve anger. Soberingly, anger is a powerful catalyst for sending damage to the third and fourth generation.

2. The Peacemaking Mediator (aka "our good child")

The peacemaking mediator is always asking, "Can't we just get along with each other?" She looks for ways to appease perpetrators in hopes of keeping the peace. Her craving for feelings of peace and normalcy inspire her to be a mediator of conflict. These peacekeeping efforts win her the title "the good girl of the family." Because she sees how her role sometimes minimizes conflict and protects everyone from more pain, her efforts seem like the right thing to do. At a deeper level, she is a pleaser. At the same time, however, she is blind to the ways that she takes on the role of an enabler. Ultimately (though not consciously), she enables her dysfunctional parents rather than confronting them.

Dysfunctional parents will often use their peacemaking mediator child as an outlet for venting anger and frustrations. Foolishly, these parents force their child to be the mature member of the family without guiding them and modeling maturity for them. They depend on their peacemaking child to act like an adult. A disturbing and surprising thing commonly happens to this child when she grows up and decides to leave home (especially if she's the older sibling). Her dysfunctional parents sometimes turn against her and resent her for leaving. They've been overly dependent on her and expected her to keep serving them so they can remain in their dysfunctional mess.

Sometimes, however, the "good girl" surprises everyone by acting out in ways that are very different from the role she took in her childhood years. Deprived of the loving guidance of mature adults has left damaging effects. Her role as peacemaker involved neglect of her own needs in exchange for meeting what she perceived to be the need of others. Essentially, she suppressed her emotions to serve the dysfunctional adults in the home and repeatedly "set herself on fire to keep everyone else warm." This experience leaves her with an empty tank. The desire to fill voids and satisfy longings makes her vulnerable to bad choices—choices seemingly out of character with the way others think of her.

Though the role of peacemaker/mediator sounds positive, it is a survival mechanism involving unhealthy approaches to conflict. While the peacemaking mediator chooses her role to protect herself and others from the destructive effects of dysfunctional adults, it doesn't lead to healthy approaches to conflict resolution. It forms ways of thinking and habits of the heart that set a child up for trouble in life—especially in future relationships.

It's sad to observe a child taking this role. She should not be blamed for any unintended consequences from doing her best to keep the peace. As she moves into adulthood, however, she will need a better understanding of the inadequacies and dangers that came with the role she filled. She must be aware of the deficiency of choosing temporary relief of conflict over honest confrontation and tough love.

When a child repeatedly chooses to escape conflict by pacifying dysfunctional adults, she sets herself up to reproduce the same behavior in other relationships. Consequently, she is vulnerable to a man who manipulates and controls her. It could also keep her from experiencing meaningful and healthy adult friendships. Her role throughout her painful upbringing damages her ability to enjoy the qualities of vulnerability, transparency, and trust.

3. The Depressed Defeatist (aka "our emotional child")

The depressed defeatist feels hopeless because of the depressing conditions of his home. Dysfunctional parents often label him as the weak or emotional child. His sadness is not taken seriously but viewed by his parents as strange and unnecessary. His dysfunctional parents are unwilling (and perhaps unable) to see how their actions create a sad life for their children. Adverse and traumatic childhood experiences make many children feel helpless and hopeless. The dysfunctional parents of the depressed defeatist will likely tell him to "snap out of it" and "learn to be thankful for the things he has."

Most likely, this child has a temperament that makes him more vulnerable to despair. Though his siblings probably understand why he feels so depressed, their temperaments keep them from the sense of defeat this child battles.

It's well-known that oppressive circumstances adversely affect neurological health. When people endure traumatic situations, their brains (the most complicated organ in the human body) sometimes underproduce necessary chemicals related to mental health. Depression is often the outcome, so we should not be surprised to hear that childhood trauma results in depressive disorder.[1] Gratefully, some helpful medications are available to assist someone struggling with depressive disorder. However, medications for depressive or anxiety disorder should be viewed as one part of a larger plan to restore health (that I discuss later in the book).

4. The Fleeing Perfectionist (aka "our trophy child")

The fleeing perfectionist tries to fill voids and meet unmet needs by turning to something that she can perfect or by consistently striving to do things the right way. If she does well enough in the eyes of her dysfunctional parents, it might win her a twisted kind of trophy status with them. She's the one the parents boast about to their friends—especially if she becomes good at something that appeals to them or gains outside recognition. For example, a fleeing perfectionist might pursue athletics with the hope of affirmation from an aloof father. Others turn to accomplishments as a means of gaining praise from teachers.

I use the word "fleeing" because the reaction is a form of escape from a dysfunctional home. This reaction is related to a child's need for realistic doses of loving affirmation to strengthen her sense of being accepted, valued, and needed. In turn, these qualities help to build a secure and healthy identity in the life of a child. Dysfunctional homes are places where the adults either neglect these needs or tear down a child's identity.

Children in dysfunctional homes are forced to live in an atmosphere of instability and uncertainty where they fend for themselves. Many of them are also forced to carry responsibilities for neglected siblings. Self-absorbed adults in these homes are too preoccupied with their issues and desires to recognize how they're damaging their children.

It's not uncommon for highly successful people to come from significantly dysfunctional backgrounds. Many well-known celebrities are among those who are reported to have come from dysfunctional upbringings. Familiar names like Oprah Winfrey, Tom Cruise, Celine Dion, Jim Carrey, Shania Twain, Leonardo DiCaprio, Demi Moore, Jay Z, Ashley Judd, Eminem, Christina Aguilera, Kelsey Grammer, and Sarah Jessica Parker are part of a list of successful celebrities with reportedly painful 18-year factors. By the same token, many famous athletes also came from dysfunctional homes.

I am not suggesting that these successful and well-known people are all fleeing perfectionists, but I suspect that each one could identify with this kind of child. In a sadly twisted irony, dysfunctional parents will show particular interest in their fleeing perfectionist if he or she becomes successful and wealthy as an adult.

When a fleeing perfectionist becomes successful and wealthy, some view it as the only redeeming thing that came from her upbringing. I am not sure I agree. On one hand, I support efforts to try to find good things about a dysfunctional home to protect your heart from bitterness. Yet, I don't believe a successful person would see her success as a redeeming value from her upbringing. Yes, she would likely agree that escaping the trap of a messed-up family played a role in fueling her motivation to become successful. However, the success itself doesn't fill the voids or heal the pain she endured during her most formative years of life.

Successful people will also tell us that their acclaim comes with a price tag that magnifies the cavities and cravings from their 18-year factor. The public tends to see a successful person as someone to aspire to emulate, and gratefully many of these people try to be positive role models for their adoring fans. In the secret places of their hearts, however, they often don't see themselves in the positive ways that their admirers do. Successful people often battle feelings of insecurity, loneliness, and even despair. Children deprived of realistic doses of loving affirmation from caring parents endure years of adult life battling such feelings—no matter how much acclaim and wealth success gives to them.

Success also intensifies struggles with intimate and healthy adult relationships. The protective mechanisms children use to survive dysfunctional homes cause them to navigate through life with larger doses of fear and distrust. Success and wealth only inspire more fear and suspicion. Regrettably, successful people must be careful about the motivations of those who want to become their friends. As a result, the qualities of vulnerability, transparency, and trust that build authentic friendships and healthy marriages become even more challenging. Though success certainly offers many positive and life-changing benefits, I am not ready to view it as a redeeming quality arising from a painful past.

I have similar hesitations regarding some recent studies that promote potential positive sides to a troubled 18-year factor. Yes, I fully affirm the ability to *leverage the pain of the past for useful purposes in the future.* Include the past in who you become instead of allowing it to define you. You cannot change the past but you can change the way the past affects the future.

Chapter 9: Evaluation and Discussion

1. Is it possible for a child to fit two of the four kinds of children described? Explain.

2. What kind of response could you picture yourself choosing to a dysfunctional home?

3. Why does the author suggest that the Angry Rebel might be the most honest one?

4. How do you think it could be beneficial to siblings who grew up in a dysfunctional home to understand the four kinds of children?

5. Many successful and wealthy people came from severely troubled homes. Why does the author hesitate to view their success as at least one good outcome from their upbringing?

6. In relation to question 5, discuss the following quote:
   A child growing up in a stable, loving home who is presented with a candy bar and told that if she waits a half hour, she can have two, would be wise to wait. But if her home is chaotic and her caregivers deliver only sporadically on their promises, it would be quite reasonable to take the candy bar while the getting is good. Grabbing what you can when it's in front of you in this context is not "impulsive" or "shortsighted," as those

behaviors are typically—and disparagingly—labeled. It's strategic.[2]

Chapter 10

Four kinds of parents

A young man asked me if I had anything in my book to help someone who had overly strict parents. I asked if that was his story. "Yes," he answered. "My mother is a very controlling person. My brother got out of the home as soon as he could because of mom's need to know everything and control everyone."

What do you remember about the way your parents raised you?

As you can imagine, their parenting approach affects your life and relationships well into adult life. Therefore, it's yet another beneficial point of evaluation in our journey. Because we tend to default to the way we were raised in our own approach, those who are currently parenting especially benefit with this evaluation.

The four approaches outlined below reflect four different kinds of parent-child relationships. Sometimes a mother will use one style and a father another. Reflect on the way your parents raised you by considering these styles.

Four approaches to parenting

1. Authoritative parents: high demand and high responsiveness

These parents set clear limits with reasonable communication. They're willing to consider legitimate compromise. They help their children understand wrong actions without being overly critical. They monitor behavior but practice age-appropriate trust for wise decisions. Children are encouraged to take responsibility for their choices and actions. Though they respect their children's feelings, they make it clear that the adults are ultimately in authority. This authoritative approach to parenting is widely considered best for children.

Results: Children are typically more capable, confident and responsible.

2. Authoritarian parents: high demand and low responsiveness

These parents use high demand with low support and little recognition. They believe children should be seen but not heard. Rules are battles for respect. These parents use a "my way or the highway" approach. Typically, they don't consider their child's feelings; they want rules followed without exception. Children are not invited to be involved in problem-solving. Discipline is what they do *to* their children not what they do *for* them. Children are made to feel bad, not encouraged to make better choices.

Results: Children tend to have low self-esteem and struggle socially. Some might become overly dependent, while others become reactionary and rebellious. Children will often choose duplicity to avoid an authoritarian parent's wrath.

3. Permissive parents: highly responsive but controlled more by the desires of children

These parents set rules, but slack on enforcement. They don't give their children a good understanding of the relationship between "action" and "consequence." They're too lenient when children need the active involvement of an adult. They too easily brush off bad behavior with clichés like "kids will be kids" and too quickly cave to a child who begs and pleads. They overplay the friend role at the expense of the parent role.

Results: Children tend to be impulsive and unrealistic about the way life works. They struggle with responsibility and show disregard for rules and people in authority. They struggle with forming peer relationships.

4. Rejecting and neglecting parents: uninvolved parents

These parents tend to be too preoccupied with their own needs, pressures, or addictions to be effective parents. Sometimes they are overwhelmed with personal and relationship problems. They don't provide proper accountability and therefore have little concern for their children's school work or whereabouts. Children don't receive the loving guidance they need for their development in maturity. Essentially, children under these kinds of parents are expected to raise themselves.

Results: Children tend to struggle with low self-worth, immaturity, and insecurity.

Unity and consistency

Sometimes parents move between different parenting styles depending on the circumstances and needs of the child. Maintaining unity and realistic consistency as parents, however, are two of the most critical factors in leading children to stable and mature adulthood. If you experienced a pronounced parenting style during your 18-year factor, it is vital to assess the effects.

Ten goals in raising children

My wife and I tried to build positive character traits into the lives of our children. We considered these traits necessary for both surviving and thriving in adult life. Because these positive traits can easily become negatives, it is important to maintain balance. We tried to be more conscious about what I call trimming the positives to protect them from the negatives.

Ten positive traits (with the negatives that threaten them)

1. Confident without being arrogant

2. Humble without being weak
3. Determined without being stubborn
4. Teachable without being gullible
5. Friendly without being naive
6. A servant without being an enabler
7. Merciful without being undiscerning
8. Discerning without being a critic
9. Capable without being overly self-reliant
10. Godly without being self-righteous

Parents who feel regret

If you regret the 18-year factor you gave your children, please consider my challenge. Make a phone call, write a letter, or have a meeting with your adult child to tell him or her what you regret. Tell them how sorry you feel for not being the mother or father you should have been. Be specific where necessary. I assure you that a conversation like this is liberating and empowering no matter the current age of your children. Be careful not to allow them to minimize your confession by telling you that you were a great dad or mom. Be courageous. No matter how uncomfortable it feels, this could be a life-changing conversation.

Chapter 10: Evaluation and Discussion

1. What kind of parents/parenting style did you experience during your 18-year factor?

2. What effects do you observe in your life as a result of the way your parents raised you?

3. What specific things did your parents do that you do not want to do as a parent?

4. Which of the ten character traits do you desire to improve upon in your life?

5. What are your thoughts about the special word to parents who regret the 18-year factor they gave their children?

DETOXING OFF
THE PAST

Do I need to go to detox?

Introduction

Raw, afraid, and nervous

In an alcohol treatment program, Diana was required to write her story. This story then afforded her a powerful visual and physical lesson about freedom from the things that bound her to a painful past.

I carried my rock

When I entered a 28-day alcohol treatment program against my will, I was given an assignment...

We were instructed to make a list of our pains: anger and things we hated...things that pushed us around. I was not ready for what happened next.

My list was a difficult thing to put on paper because writing these things down made them feel real. Once it was in print, I could not wash them away, medicate them or push them down into my heart anymore. Exposing the painful things in my life made me feel raw, afraid, and nervous. It felt much safer to keep these things to myself. I couldn't trust others with my personal pain. What would they think of me if I told the truth about my life? I had become accustomed to the fears and anger from all the things that had happened to me: having a parent that was a bingeing alcoholic, being the object of sexual abuse in our house, being gang-raped on the way to church camp, of all places.

Everything seemed even more unbearable because I could find no one to talk to; nowhere to unburden my troubled heart. I battled a range of emotions from anger to shame to fear. Another difficulty was the fact that my family was highly regarded in the county in which I lived. The few times I sought out treatment when I started with my family history, or just said my full name, the response always seemed the same: "Oh, you're so and so's daughter," or "Oh, I know your parents." That ended the session because I feared to let others know the truth about my family. I stuffed all the troubles more deeply in my soul and left the office.

After getting the courage to write down all the pains... anger and things I hated...things that pushed me around, we went out on an activity with our lists in hand. We went to a park and were instructed to find a rock and show it to the counselor. We then took our list and with rubber bands bound them to our rocks. Then, in a heartfelt moment, we were told to toss them over the bridge into the stream, never to be bothered by these things again. Well, not so for me.

The counselor did not like my rock and told me to find another one. Off I went only to have the next rock rejected. "No," my counselor said, "find a bigger rock." I was finally instructed to find a rock that required two hands for carrying back. I became frustrated and wanted to stop this meaningless game. After I found a very heavy rock that was acceptable, the rubber bands were not big enough for attaching my list to it. Out came the duct tape instead. I proceeded to the bridge area to hurl my "rock" over the edge with my list duct taped to it. The counselor stopped me. He told me to carry my rock back with me. In the group, in front of everybody, he gave me these special instructions. I was to carry my rock with me 24/7.

Great! I tried to set the rock on the seat next to me. "No," I was told, "that was not the instruction." I was to carry my rock with me on my lap, on my food tray, on my bed...every place I went I had to carry this rock. Well, it seemed to get heavier and heavier. The counselors knew that I was in a deep state of denial and they were determined to bring me to the truth.

On day three, the light came on, the floodgates of my heart opened. I rang the bell like I never had before; this [bell] was always there to let everybody know that you were ready to expose something, to let something out, to unburden your heart.

Everybody came to the group, and in a very uncharacteristic flood of emotions, through tears, with anger and clenched fists, I put the "rock" in the center of the circle. I then almost in an uncontrollable way began to shout out all these things on my list. My anger and fears were NOT GOING TO BE CARRIED AROUND anymore. The more I screamed out these things, the lighter I felt. Exhausted, I fell to a heap on the floor. I could not move. I looked at everybody; no one was mad at me, no one hated me, no one pushed me away. Instead, they embraced me, wiped away my tears. They were given special instructions too. Each person was to whisper a special word or tell me a special gift they would give me.

I only remember two things—life changing things. I heard whispered [to me] so soft and gentle, "I am proud of you" and "You matter." The counselor then gave me a gift of sorts. He gave me a little ceremonial tree. It was my job to water it, take care of it, and it would grow tall and strong. I slept for about three days with the encouraging words and ideas about this ceremonial tree swimming around my head. When I graduated [after] the 28 days, the counselor promised me I never had to carry "that rock" around. He also told me that if I ever felt the need to pick up a "rock," to stop and pick up the sapling and take care of it, nurture it and watch it grow. I was that sapling; I needed to grow tall and strong.

It is good to look back at these things, to cease being pushed around, burdened by the past, to know that they are memories. I do not need to carry them around or relive them anymore. Now, so many years later, the only rocks I pick up are the kind you can skip across a lake or pond. They skip with joy and pleasure, seemingly to dance over the water.

The journey ahead

Overcoming the harmful effects of a toxic upbringing is not an outpatient procedure. After spending time in the Detox Unit, we will move to the Operating Room, then to Recovery and Rehab.

Chapter 11

Welcome to detox

I learned many years ago that I could not help an alcoholic get to a better place unless he first went through detox. Purging toxicity is not an easy process. Physical detox off drugs or alcohol addiction can be an excruciating experience. It involves sweating, changes in bodily temperature, shaking and convulsing, excessive yawning, gripping anxiety, irritation, agitation, aggressiveness, self-harm, efforts to harm others, muscle pain, delirium, watery eyes, runny nose, insomnia and more.[1]

Does detoxing seem like an extreme analogy for the process needed to overcome a troubled upbringing? Consider how the word "toxic" has recently become a common term for describing people and relationships. "Toxic" is an adjective describing something as poisonous, harmful, and unsafe. We think of toxic waste or water or even toxic debt. By the same token, toxic homes are unsafe places that are harmful to children. I am using this word to refer to toxic emotions and toxic ways of thinking that are at the root of toxic relationships. These toxins do not appear without a history.

Toxic upbringing

Growing up in a toxic home causes a child's heart to become a holding tank of harmful emotions and unsafe ways of thinking. Such homes put a child at risk of being dangerous to himself and to others—of spreading toxicity. It's difficult for healthy lives and relationships to come from toxic hearts. The child who grows up in this kind of home will likely need some detox before he can do well in adult life and relationships.

I am using the illustration of detox as a process of identifying, tracking and purging the toxic effects of a troubled past.

I don't need detox!

Resistance to detox is normal. A detox unit is scary. People with a painful past sometimes prefer to hide. They choose a life of isolation, insulation, and victimization. It feels safer to hide. As Diana admitted, "Exposing the painful things in my life made me feel raw, afraid, and nervous. It felt much safer to keep these things to myself. I couldn't trust others with my pain. What would they think of me if I told the truth about my life?" Trusting others with her pain seemed like a risky thing to do. It feels safer to do what is ultimately unsafe.

The duplicity of living as two people is exhausting and destructive. In detox we're saying that it's time to stop trying to wash away, medicate, or push down the things that make life toxic. To survive a troubled upbringing, children learn to bottle up toxic thinking and emotions. This protective instinct, however, is very disruptive and harmful to adult life and relationships. Sooner or later a painful past has a way of making itself known in ways that are far more painful than confronting it now. Don't wait for this to happen. Confront yourself now.

Four essential steps in detox

Purging the toxic effects of a painful past involves at least four steps.
1. Revisit the past.
2. Return responsibility to the abuser(s).
3. Reject a victim mentality.
4. Require boundaries.

1. Revisit the past: write your story

Everyone benefits from writing their story. Those who grew up in healthy homes benefit because they don't always have a clear understanding of how their upbringing affected their lives. In a relationship, two people who came from healthy homes also came from *different* homes, and differences can be a source of significant conflict. When we try to form and enjoy close relationships, different backgrounds have a way of making life challenging. Rather than waiting for a difficult relationship to cause you to think about ways your upbringing affected your life, I suggest that you write your story now. Writing your story is a means through which you track the sources behind emotions and ways of thinking. We cannot change what we don't understand.

Those who survived a troubled upbringing especially need to write their story, although it will likely be more difficult for them. First, victims of traumatic childhood experiences tend to dismiss or minimize what happened to them. It just feels less threatening to pretend nothing too severe happened during a troubled upbringing. Secondly, as we mentioned before, children also tend to misread what happens *to them* as something wrong *with them*. This tendency carries on in adult life with false ownership of blame for trauma from the past. Self-blame obscures the truth about the past and binds a victim to a painful future.

The path to a better future begins with restoring the truth about what happened during childhood years and refusing to blame yourself for the actions of dysfunctional and abusive adults. Writing your story is restoring the truth and reality about your past.

Diana felt terrified by the assignment of writing a list of her pains: anger and things she hated...things that pushed her around. She said, "My list was a difficult thing to put on paper because [it] made them feel real...I could not wash them away, medicate them or push them down into my heart anymore. I felt raw, afraid, and nervous to expose the painful things in my life." With her unhealthy approval addiction, Abigail (in chapter eight) confessed, "tears are rolling down my face as I am writing my story."

The thought of taking a written trip down memory lane could make you feel raw, afraid and nervous. It might also involve tears. It's a process of confronting and purging the toxic feelings and ways of thinking. It will take courage to overcome the fear that deceives us into thinking that it's safer to suppress painful feelings and hide bad memories.

Perhaps we understand toxic emotions when we feel them, but it's when we put our feelings into words and complete sentences that we can honestly appraise ourselves. An evaluation of ourselves is incomplete without the use of specific words to describe our upbringing. Remember that this assignment is not an invitation to wallow in self-pity or fill your heart with anger, but to provide a means for moving to a better place.

Write specifically about your father, mother, or other adults who affected you. Write out the ways your upbringing impacted your emotions and ways of thinking. Acknowledge the things that make you become defensive or tempt you to shut down. Make a list of your pains: anger and things you hated...things that pushed you around. Look closely at the walls and defense mechanisms you use. Why do you choose, for example, to be cynical? Why do you use sarcastic humor?

Overcoming a problem involves understanding *where* and *how* it originated. Writing your story is an essential step toward this understanding. We must track the accurate sources behind toxic emotions, ways of thinking, and ways of reacting. Think of this assignment as a means for confronting things that are poisoning your life and relationships.

"Dèyè mòn, gen mòn." This Haitian proverb translates, "Behind mountains, more mountains."[2] It's a picturesque way of saying there's a story behind the story. So, in the words of preservationist John Muir, "The mountains are calling, and I must go, and I will work on while I can."[3] Although I caution you not to be too absorbed with your past, I am equally concerned about being too casual about it.

Self-perception is often cloudy because suppression and denial play a significant role in a troubled upbringing. As you write about your 18-year factor, give yourself time to process the emotions, but don't allow anything to keep you from pressing on into the mountains behind your mountain.

If a writing assignment feels intimidating, find a trusted and wise friend or counselor who can help you with the task. Tell this person your story but allow them to take written notes of specific things that you'll need to revisit in the recovery room. A worksheet for writing or telling your story is available in Appendix I.

2. Return responsibility to the abuser(s)

Self-blame for traumatic childhood experiences must end. Parents, guardians, or other adults who neglect or abuse children will sometimes shift blame for the abuse onto the child. They might say, "If you weren't such a difficult kid, you could have had a better life" or "Don't you think you brought it on yourself?" or "Half of your problems were your own doing."

Self-blame, a toxic effect of a troubled 18-year factor, is often the basis for a self-limiting belief system children carry from their traumatic experiences into adulthood. Self-doubt plays a significant role in shaping a child's mind because of the lies and deceptions that were "normal" to his upbringing. One of the most formidable lies is self-blame for experiences under dysfunctional adults. We must detox this harmful effect by being very clear that we're not given a choice about the kind of upbringing we experience or the adults who raise us. Many understandably resent this fact. Most, however, retain some degree of self-blame for their upbringing.

Returning responsibility to an abuser should purge the toxicity of self-blame for a lousy upbringing. At its core, it's a step toward purging the damaging messages sent by abusive parents or other adults.

It's time to stop making excuses for the hurtful actions of abusers. I am asking you to make a verbal and written transfer of responsibility to the adults responsible for your 18-year factor. Name the adults and the specific ways they hurt you. Remind yourself that these things were not experiences chosen by you and that you are not at fault. Resolve not to allow others to make you feel responsible or guilty for the actions and words of adult abusers, recognizing that you were the victim. To be clear, I'm not inviting you to play the blame-game or to become angry and bitter. These kinds of reactions extend victimhood and bind you to the abusers. Don't be surprised, however, at unexpected emotions when you make a verbal and written transfer of responsibility. Removing self-blame is emotionally challenging. You are wise to take this step with the help of a trusted friend or counselor.

3. Reject a victim mentality

It's one thing to accept that you were a victim of the actions of others (step two); it's another to choose a victim mentality that gives the pain from the past control over the present. Feelings of helplessness often accompany childhood trauma, but you are not helpless as an adult. Though you cannot go back and change the past, you can change the way it affects your present life. Others caused your pain, but your healing is your responsibility.

Remaining in perpetual victimhood will chain you to a life controlled by an abuser. The powerful lure of self-pity invites victims of trauma to mentalities of defeat and victimhood. It's not easy to reclaim control of your life, but freedom from a painful past involves a strange combination of accepting that you were a victim and rejecting a victim mentality. This purging process will be painful for those who see victimhood as necessary for justified access to certain forms of redress. They don't understand how a victim mentality, one which waits until the other person changes/confesses/asks forgiveness, postpones a better future. One adult with a dysfunctional father argued, "I'll stop being resentful when he apologizes."

"What if he never apologizes?" I asked. Conditioning your changes on another person changing binds you to ongoing adverse effects of the neglect or abuse.

- The only person you can change is you.
- Transfer responsibility for the past to the adults but take responsibility for the present.
- Where you've been doesn't have to define who you become.
- Include the past in who you become instead of letting it determine who you are.
- The only thing you can change about the past is how it affects the future.

The damage we experienced as children remains in control of our lives when we refuse to see ourselves as responsible and significant.

When one observes the rifts and scars of children whose parents took turns slapping, deriding, ignoring, bullying, or, sometimes worse, simply abandoning them; when one observes the wholesale life mismanagement of grown-ups who have lived for years in the shadow of their bereft childhood and who have attempted with one addictor after another to fill up those empty places where love should have settled, only to discover that their addictor keeps enlarging the very void it was meant to fill—when one knows people of this kind and observes their largely predictable character pathology, one hesitates to call all this chaos sin. The label sounds smug and impertinent. In such cases, we want to appeal to some broader category, perhaps the category of tragedy.

"Tragedy" implies the fall of someone who is responsible and significant. It refers to someone whose significance has been "compromised and crushed by a mix of forces, including personal agency, that work together for evil in a way that seems simultaneously surprising and predictable, preventable and inevitable." A tragic figure is, in some intricate combination, both weak and willful, both foolish and guilty.

Remarkably enough, at the end of the day, it might not matter very much how we classify damaging behavior. Whether these behaviors amount to sin or symptom, the prescription for dealing with them may turn out to be just about the same. Nobody, for example, is more insistent than Alcoholics Anonymous that alcoholism is a disease; nobody is more insistent than A.A. on the need for the alcoholic to take full responsibility for his disease and deal with it in brutal candor.[4]

4. Require boundaries

Removing toxicity almost always requires boundaries to protect you from the people who caused the toxicity. A wife and mother said, "Whenever I go to visit my mother for a week, everyone braces for my return. They know it will take me a few weeks to get to a better place after spending time with my mom."

"Is mom that toxic?" I asked.

"Oh yes!" she answered.

"Why do you put yourself and everyone else through this experience?" Perhaps you could guess how she answered me.

"She is my mother, and it seems wrong to not visit with her." I've heard this same scenario far too many times. Why isn't wrong assigned to the person who is responsible for spreading toxicity? Why do adult children take responsibility for the toxic behaviors of their immature, manipulative, and controlling parents? We must purge the toxicity of self-imposed guilt and misguided responsibility.

Boundaries are especially essential when toxic parents are causing trouble for an adult child's marriage. When a spouse observes the one they love pushed around, it ignites protective instincts that could lead to more difficulty. Boundaries can protect against the escalation of trouble. When boundaries are necessary, it's wise to write an explanation for why limits are needed, what they involve, what is not intended by the boundaries, and what happens when disrespected.

In Lisa's story from the introduction to chapter four, she shared how she had reached a point where she only saw her father once in five years because he became too volatile to be near. During her last visit with her father, she recalled,

All the anger and rage that I always felt from him, but never saw, came out. He screamed and cursed and called my children obscene names and almost hit my son. He even grabbed my husband by the face and screamed at him. It was terrifying. But it was also a relief to finally see the thing I'd been afraid of for all those years. To know it wasn't just in my head. It was real. What I saw that day was exactly what I'd felt my entire life instinctively.

It's notable that Lisa's terrifying final encounter with her father gave her relief. Why? Because it confirmed for her the truth about what she felt throughout her life. Mixed with her relief is another subtle freedom from carrying responsibility for her father and feeling guilty for not visiting him.

I've also witnessed an opposite reaction in which some children resent their parents so much that they want nothing to do with them. Both choices are unhealthy ways of relating to toxic parents. The first choice makes the mistake of assuming ownership for parents beyond healthy limits; the second choice strangely allows parents to sit in the control room of the heart.

It's time to require adults to act like adults. I don't have much patience for selfish, immature, and demanding adults who act more like children than their children. If boundaries are needed with parents or other adults, I suggest putting them in place based on clear communication that transfers responsibility for the boundary to the parent or other adults.

The wife and mother above could say or write the following to her mother, "Mom, I love you, and I am grateful for you as my mother. I want to visit with you, but I need to be honest about the effects it has on my life." She must be specific about the toxic behaviors, speech, and attitudes that affect her. If she courageously and wisely communicates these things, she will likely need to brace for an immature, angry and manipulative reaction. When this happens, she must refuse to take the bait by becoming argumentative. Defuse rather than infusing. De-escalate instead of escalating. Use purposeful silence; tell mom you're disappointed in her reaction and affirm your hope that she will see a need for changes that would make her life and your relationship much healthier. We cannot detox off of toxic emotions, thoughts, and actions by remaining in the close company of those who caused the toxicity.

Chapter 11: Evaluation and Discussion

1. What did you find insightful or helpful in Diana's story, "I carried my rock"?

2. What does the author intend in the use of the illustration of detox?

3. Why are some people resistant to detox?

4. Why does the author consider it helpful to write the story of our upbringing?

5. Summarize the primary purpose in writing down your story.

6. How do the steps of returning responsibility to an abuser and rejecting a victim mentality relate to each other?

7. Why is it sometimes necessary to use boundaries with toxic adults?

8. Have you had any experiences with boundaries?

9. Make a list of toxic emotions, thoughts or actions that connect with your upbringing.

Chapter 12

Welcome to the O. R.
(Not an outpatient procedure)

After completing detox, we go to the O. R. (Operating Room). Surgery is necessary, and the first two cuts are the deepest. After undergoing surgery, we need a plan for recovery that will take us to a better place.

First surgical cut: unexpected damage from a troubled past

We must surgically remove unexpected damage from your troubled upbringing. That unexpected damage is a protective mechanism common to all children who grew up in dysfunctional homes. I am surprised by how little attention this consequence receives.

I've made this surgical cut many times after people have told me their story of a painful and challenging childhood. At the start, I prep for the surgical incision by telling them that I am very sorry that they endured so much trouble and pain under the people who should have loved and cared for them. With genuine care, I say to them that I wish I could go back in time and start their lives over again with a healthy home, though we all know that this is impossible. I encourage them to be confident that they can get to a better place by changing the way their past affects their future. Life does not have to be forever controlled by a troubled upbringing.

Then I make the surgical cut by assuring them that they will never get to a better place and put the pain of their past behind them until they recognize a truth that will not be easy for me to tell them and perhaps very difficult for them to hear. They look at me with intensity as I say, "One of the more destructive effects of your painful past is the reality that **YOU matter to YOU far too much.**"

I understand that you didn't matter to the people who should have valued and protected you. Their failure caused you to have to look out for yourself; it was a survival mechanism. This childhood instinct is harmful to adulthood—especially relationships. It's the disease of being self-absorbed in the hurts of yesterday. Strangely, those who experienced neglect or abuse become self-destructive by being self-focused in unhealthy ways. This is the primary hindrance keeping them from experiencing freedom from their past.

Freedom comes when we recycle the pain and leverage it to help others. Detox is necessary for feeling healthy enough to help others. Self-absorbed sadness over our losses will lead to a life of self-limited fear and self-protective control. We will find ourselves retreating from threats and dangers that don't exist as we keep others at a distance.

Look up. Look around. Whom do you see who could benefit from what you experienced? Venture out a little and live outside of yourself. Remind yourself often and reflect deeply on the unexpected outcome of a troubled past that YOU MATTER TO YOU FAR TOO MUCH. Although it's important to look closely at the effects of the past and to process the ways it affects our lives and relationships, it's equally essential not to *remain* focused on the past. The object of our focus often becomes our reality. Freedom is not found in a life that keeps me at the center.

Second surgical cut: removing a cancerous growth— unforgiveness.

When unforgiveness is left to grow, it attaches to the destructive emotions of resentment, anger, and bitterness (cherished resentments). Forgiveness (not revenge) is the only antivenom for the venom of bitterness. In a documentary on the Holocaust, a survivor of the Warsaw ghetto uprising talked about the bitterness that remains in his soul over how the Nazis treated him and his neighbors: "If you could lick my heart," he says, "it would poison you."[1]

Extensive (and relatively recent) research into the effects of forgiveness reveals that the Holocaust survivor's self-assessment is "more than metaphorical." Millions of dollars of research funding devoted to a study of the impact of forgiveness led social scientists to conclude that forgiveness is essential to a victim's emotional and physical wellbeing. The benefits of forgiveness include release from anger, rage, and stress—emotions associated with physiological problems such as hypertension, high blood pressure, cardiovascular diseases, and psychosomatic conditions.[2]

There's likely a connection between the findings regarding forgiveness and the research from The Adverse Childhood Experiences (ACE) Study.[3] This study demonstrates a strong relationship between childhood trauma and physical and emotional health. Physical, emotional or psychological trauma (deeply distressing and painful experiences) during an 18-year factor overwhelm children with stressful feelings of helplessness and hopelessness in ways that do not disappear in adulthood. Resentment and anger are also common responses to adverse childhood experiences. It's possible to be hurt so badly that you feel buried under emotions from a painful past.

Forgiveness is not always easy when someone is hurt badly. In such cases, it sounds cheap when people talk about the need to "forgive and forget." Most people don't want anything to do with forgiveness if it means swallowing hard and letting an offender off the hook or pretending the offense wasn't that bad. Though it often feels right to remain unforgiving toward an offender, an unforgiving heart is difficult to endure; it will ultimately keep you from experiencing freedom and a better future.

An unforgiving heart thrives upon the delicious, deceptive, and destructive emotions of anger, resentment, and bitterness. They are *delicious* because injured people desire retaliation. Emotional retaliation (resenting and hating the one who hurt us) is a more accessible substitute for actual revenge. They are *deceptive* because we feel we have a right to the emotions that blind and bind us to their effects. Resentment indicates a level of emotional connection with the reality of a painful past. Though that emotional connection could be a catalyst to freedom, it lures us with a false feeling of control. Ultimately, feelings of resentment can only lead to freedom and true control if processed based on an accurate understanding of forgiveness. Finally, these emotions are *destructive* when given a home in our hearts because they always corrupt the container that carries them. Nothing good grows in hearts that are angry, resentful, and bitter. Bitter people are infectious. Bitterness doubles loss and extends the effects to others.

We cannot experience a better future unless we change the way we view our cherished resentments. They are roadblocks to freedom. Holding things against others is a deceptive way of holding onto the one who hurt us. It helps to understand three things forgiveness is *not*.

1. Forgiveness is not an act of condoning the wrongs of an abuser. It's a choice to reject a cancerous grudge that will destroy your life.
2. Forgiveness is not a one-time act. People say, "forgive and forget" as if it's an easy thing to do. Forgiveness is often a decision that requires many reaffirmations.
3. Forgiveness is not reconciliation. Don't assume that forgiving requires immediate reconciliation. It might open the door to the possibility of restoring a relationship, but the notion that forgiveness and reconciliation must happen simultaneously is one of the main reasons people remain trapped in unforgiveness. Forgiveness does not require an offended party to immediately treat an offender as if he did no wrong.

Reconciliation (understood as distinct from forgiveness) could involve enforcement of healthy and natural consequences. Restoring a broken relationship might include restitution, a period of detachment, and new boundaries for the relationship. When understood as a process distinct from forgiveness, it helps people feel free to forgive.

When hesitant to reconcile, an abuser might resort to manipulation by labeling you "unforgiving." He must be informed, however, that he's *confusing forgiveness and reconciliation.* Restoring trust (when deeply or repeatedly violated) is a matter that requires changes in the one who hurt us. However, be careful not to withhold reconciliation over minor grievances or as a means of retaliation. This withholding allows bitterness (and our offender) to remain in control.

Replacing toxic relationships

Even recovery requires a difficult step: replacing toxic relationships with healthy ones. Does anyone go in the wrong direction without running with others? It's equally difficult to move in the right direction alone.

A primary reason people remain stuck in their dysfunction is because they choose to commiserate with miserable people who share similar stories of trouble. Indeed, it might feel a little scary to connect with healthy people, but you need them. You can find caring and compassionate people who won't look down on you for a difficult upbringing you did not choose.

Call to those with healthy childhoods

Allow me to reaffirm a call to those who had a healthy upbringing. If you experienced a healthy and functionally stable childhood, you received a gift that has become increasingly rare. Write a thank you note to those responsible. A rapidly growing number of people have a very different story. These

166

people battle with regrets, bad memories, and/or losses that keep them from enjoying each new day. They might understand that remaining stuck in the sorrows and pain of yesterday prevents them from experiencing the wonders of today and hope for a better tomorrow. However, they often don't know where to begin to find freedom. Consider being part of a team to help someone trying to overcome the effects of a painful past.

Reaffirming the good things

For those who endured the painful childhood, I challenge you to reaffirm the good things you learned as a child. It is unhealthy to be too one-sided in our perspective. Find something to affirm from your upbringing even if it's only the food and shelter provided for you. Then, reaffirm what you learned through the difficult experiences. Accentuating the positives will help you think more clearly and objectively about other matters from your past. One woman told me that freedom for her began when she gave thanks for her alcoholic father and asked God to use her experiences to help others.

Renouncing toxic ways of thinking

Significantly disrupted or severely dysfunctional 18-year factors leave deep tracks in our hearts and minds. These thought patterns and heart postures deserve close examination. We must repeatedly renounce wrong and hurtful ways of thinking about ourselves, life, and others.

A troubled upbringing often causes many wrong ways of thinking. We must confront the false perceptions that put us in the hospital (self-blame or guilt, self-doubt, self-loathing, paralyzing feelings of insecurity, reading threats where they don't exist, efforts to control everything, and over-generalizations about all men or all women). Repeated emphasis on these perceptions further solidifies the wrong thinking. When these ways of thinking emerge, confront yourself; speak to yourself about a better way to think. Stop listening to yourself and start speaking to yourself.

If feelings of self-blame for your upbringing emerge, verbally assign responsibility to those to whom it belongs. Confront your unwillingness to trust others or your need to control others, or your desire to be self-sufficient—needing no one! Accept that life in this world is vulnerable. Unhealthy fear of vulnerability will keep you from allowing your heart to love another person. Choosing to love others always involves risk of being hurt, but painful experiences can be a means to growth. Recognize how fear of loss or betrayal destroy your ability to enjoy loving relationships.

Identifying and overcoming destructive thought patterns is essential for getting to a better place. It doesn't happen quickly because it's not a one-time act. Persistence, patience, and resolve are necessary. The process usually requires the help of others for gaining new ways of seeing things.

Keep notes regarding the way you perceive things and people. Take special note of things that trigger your thoughts. Be persistent in interrupting your internal dialogue by correcting wrong ways of thinking. I reiterate, stop listening to yourself and start speaking to yourself. Sometimes the positive emotion helps us overcome the destructive emotion. Affection, for example, cancels out aggression. Acceptance and hope do the same to sadness and anxiety.

Replacing overgeneralized negative labels

If your parent repeatedly told you that you are stupid, the counteracting truth is not to tell yourself that you're not stupid. We all do dumb things. There's a big difference, however, between doing stupid things and being labeled "stupid." Recognize the difference between a label and an occasional action. Establishing a new way of thinking is not replacing overgeneralized negative labels with overgeneralized positive ones. Hyped-up positive labels replace one lie for another. We must learn to be comfortably realistic about ourselves. Recognize, use, and be thankful for your strengths. Don't exaggerate or dramatize your weaknesses. Learning to laugh at ourselves helps to build a healthy identity.

New ways of thinking

Allow yourself time for getting to a better place. It is a process that requires patience and involves learning new ways of thinking and new habits.

- Do not allow yesterday's regrets or tomorrow's fears destroy the progress of each day.
- Confront your tendencies.
- Discipline yourself.
- Celebrate small victories and turn them into life habits.
- You might not be where you want to be but be encouraged when you're not where you used to be. Progress can feel like three steps forward and two back. The important thing is to never give up.
- Connect with a specific (and healthy) accountability partner.
- Ask those who are close to you to be patient as you make progress on a path to a better future.

Chapter 12: Evaluation and Discussion

1. Why does the author consider the first surgical cut to be "unexpected damage from a troubled past"?

2. How did the words "YOU MATTER TO YOU FAR TOO MUCH" impact you?

3. Why is the first surgical cut essential to a better future?

4. What are some of the effects of unforgiveness?

5. Summarize the delicious, deceptive, and destructive effects of unforgiveness.

6. What is the difference between forgiveness and reconciliation and why is it essential to understand it?

7. What are the three things that forgiveness is not?

8. Why is it important yet difficult to replace toxic relationships with healthy ones?

9. List some of the good things you learned during your 18-year factor.

10. Summarize some of the points you found helpful under "Renouncing toxic ways of thinking."

11. Why are positive statements not always useful for counteracting negative labels?

Chapter 13

Welcome to Recovery and Rehab
(Restoring the whole person)

There are significant downstream social and physical effects of adverse childhood experiences. Perhaps the most extensive supporting research is the Adverse Childhood Experiences (ACE) study, which I mentioned in the prior chapter. The study particularly challenges long-standing assumptions that childhood trauma leads to higher health risks because traumatized children engage in high-risk behaviors. Compelling evidence now suggests that the childhood trauma itself (apart from high-risk behaviors) indicates greater chances of developing a variety of health problems in adult life.

Restoration is not one-dimensional

Undoubtedly, humans are multidimensional beings. Far too often, our needs are treated with one-dimensional remedies. Restoration efforts must focus on our whole person.

Conversation with my medical doctor
(biologically-disordered depression)

Comment from my doctor:
> Sometimes I diagnose what I believe to be biologically-based depression and I give a patient a prescription for antidepressants, only to have the patient go to a spiritual advisor who then counsels them with a "five-Bible-verses-and-you'll-be-better" prescription.

My response:
> I get it, doc. It's wrong for these spiritual advisors to reduce people to purely spiritual beings who simply need more Bible verses. However, I am sure that you agree that we equally should not reduce people to merely physical beings with only neurological needs. The primary prescriber of antidepressants and anti-anxiety medications are you and your fellow family practitioners. I understand that you have a list of nine characteristics for assessing depression, but my concern is how quickly a diagnosis is possible and how misleading it could be to think of the medicine as the remedy.
> By the way, how much time do you spend with each patient? If I get ten minutes of your time, it seems like a lot. You have patients waiting in other rooms. How

adequately can a diagnosis be made in such a short amount of time? And how often do we misdiagnose normal sadness as disordered sadness? Don't misunderstand. I sympathize with the pressures on doctors ever since the unseating of therapeutic psychology by bio-psychology. I realize that the convergence of medicine with pharmacology, insurance, lawyers, and big business has made work complicated for doctors. I am also grateful for the benefits of drugs for neurologically related needs.

My concern is how often a patient assumes that medicine is the whole answer for her needs. Is consideration given to her social circumstances? We are also social beings with relationship needs. Perhaps we also have unrealistic expectations for happiness. Do we have an adequate understanding of the anatomy of normal sadness and how it differs from disordered depression?

Holistic restoration: remedies focused on four dimensions of life

Humans are...
1. Physical beings with bodily needs
2. Social beings with relationship needs
3. Psychological beings with cognitive needs.
4. Spiritual beings with spiritual needs

Restoration must involve remedies that respect an integration of the physical, social, psychological, and spiritual parts of life with respect to the three primary expressions of personhood.

1. Intellect: our minds (thoughts, imagination)

2. Emotion: our feelings (affections)
3. Will: our choices (decision-making)

Consider a few thoughts under each of the four dimensions in relation with the three expressions of personhood.

1. Physical restoration

We are more than our genes and our brain chemistry, yet we are significantly affected by both. There's a good bit of evidence demonstrating ways that adverse and traumatic childhood experiences alter the brain of a child. The brain (arguably our most complicated organ) will under-respond and over-respond during traumatic or intensely stressful experiences.[1]

I once asked a neurophysiologist, who happens to be a good friend of many years, if the brain's neurochemistry will change when a person endures traumatic experiences. I anticipated that he would affirm this to be true. My next question is most important to me. "When a person gets to a healthier place," I asked, "is it possible for the brain to be restored to its normal function? His affirmative answer supported my counseling experience with people who needed medicinal aid to help them get to "a better place" but felt they did not need the medicine when life became much healthier. I never recommend discontinuing medication without consulting a medical doctor, but a growing list of people with whom I work made this choice and are doing well.

We must respect the physical dimension and its effects on other parts of life. For example, you shouldn't wait for a doctor to tell you that you need to change the way you eat or that you need to get more sleep or more exercise. Build positive habits in these areas now. Personally, I know that I feel better, think more clearly, and process emotions in a more healthy way when I am physically active, eating well and getting adequate rest. Balancing the various dimensions of life requires daily discipline. Though I often find that I need to force myself to exercise and to make wise decisions about what I eat, it's worth the effort. Learning when to say "yes" and "no" is a big part of this balance.

2. Social restoration: relationships and life's circumstances

Our sociology (relationships/circumstances) plays a significant role in shaping our lives and must be taken seriously by those who counsel a person holistically.

Most people desire loving and lasting relationships. Why then do the majority of marriages fail? They either end in separation and divorce or become dysfunctional and unhappy relationships of complacency and distance. What has doomed us to such extensive failure? Have we overlooked anything that might help us live happily ever after?

I believe that what is happening with marriages is due in part to the pervasive effects of dysfunctional homes. Children who endure troubled upbringings hunger for healthy relationships, yet they struggle to find and enjoy them. Is it possible that an unhealthy sense of identity and security resulting from their troubled past causes them to sabotage adult relationships?

Self-doubt and self-limited beliefs

Significant adverse experiences during childhood years produce a variety of forms of self-doubt. Though these doubts are typically more subconscious than conscious, they still cause trouble in adult relationships. Perhaps (at a subconscious level) we feel we're not worth loving and therefore feel insecure with others. Our insecurity unintentionally sabotages a relationship when it shows up as guardedness, defensiveness, or an obsessive need for affirmation.

A child who grows up in a dysfunctional home develops a self-limiting belief system that is not always apparent on the surface. Their belief system puts them on alert to troubles that exist more in their minds due to their past than they do in reality. Detecting threats that do not exist, they become unnecessarily stressed in places that are safe. They leave their childhood years still surveying life for risks and dangers whether imagined or real. The doubts and damaged self-belief system developed during the early years often operate as an unrecognized source of relationship difficulty. Cycles of alarm and fear and the efforts to control continually result in misinterpretations, second-guessing, and misunderstandings. It all plays out in ways that make it difficult for love to grow. These experiences put unnecessary stress on relationships in ways that suffocate them or siphon the life out of them.

Redirecting blame

The complication involved in loving and supporting people with a damaged self-belief system is more difficult because of a common tendency to redirect blame to the one who loves them rather than to the ones who initially hurt them. It's hard to build a healthy relationship on a foundation of self-doubt, insecurity and self-alienating emotions and actions.

The unknown and unintentional parts of this assault on relationships can be removed by looking more closely at ways our upbringing caused them. Use the 26 questions in Appendix II for evaluating the effects of your 18-year factor on current relationships.

Simplify and Prioritize

Regarding the effects of circumstances on our lives, constant efforts are necessary for simplifying and prioritizing life in ways that help to reduce stress. Determination not to be controlled by the expectations or manipulation of others will likely be part of stress reduction.

3. Psychological restoration: choosing to see things differently

Researchers indicate that children with high levels of exposure to adversity are at greater risk of developing mental disorders. The more common disorders include anxiety, depression, learning disabilities, aggressive behaviors, and a variety of phobias. Adverse neurological and cognitive effects of childhood trauma are also known to cast a long shadow over adult life.[2] The breadth of findings on this matter paints a less than encouraging picture.

While it's beyond debate that traumatic childhood experiences result in adverse physical effects on neurological health, it's important to remind ourselves that we are more than physical beings with physical needs. There is a need for more research focused on integrating cognitive and emotional effects. Connecting thinking and feelings might offer surprising help for more holistic restoration.

Feelings and thinking

177

Children tend to bury their feelings when they endure a troubled home. However, they don't remain buried; they reemerge in ways that disturb adult life—especially relationships. Many adults wish they could stop battling negative feelings that linger from a difficult childhood. The critical (and misunderstood) fact is that lasting change in the way I *feel* (my emotion), or for that matter, in what I *do* (my will), only occurs when I change the way I *think*. Of the three expressions of personhood, the intellect (our mind, thoughts, perspectives, imagination) is foundational.

The social dimension is also involved. The people around us play a role in perspective formation. If we commiserate with miserable people, we should not be surprised that we remain miserable. Children learn to see things based on the influences of others during their 18-year factor. These influences involve parents, cultural expectations, and other experiences (both positive and negative). Challenging and changing harmful ways of thinking often necessitates the aforementioned boundaries to protect us from those who exert forceful influence on our perspectives.

Consider two illustrations.

Discouragement

Consider as an illustration the need to discourage a discouraged person. Sound strange? We need to discourage her from the way of thinking that traps her in feelings of discouragement. Discouragement notoriously and selectively focuses on some parts of life and overlooks others. Perspective/outlook is the key to many changes in life. The way we view or construe things lies behind our feelings and actions (positively or negatively) to fortify our emotions and decision-making.

Anger

Getting to a better place requires an understanding of the relationship between thinking, emotions, and actions. Consider a child raised in a home where he learned that anger is an emotion to suppress. He thinks that we are not supposed to feel angry. Suppression, however, is not a healthy way to process anger; indeed, sometimes anger is an appropriate response. Conversely, a child who grew up only witnessing unhealthy and violent expressions of anger might believe it is an emotion to avoid. These children must unlearn their wrong ways of thinking about anger and learn to express this important emotion in healthy ways. Internalizing and suppressing anger leads to a variety of negative physical and relationship issues.

We experience anger as an emotion that connects to things we consider important. Children whose parents either taught them that anger is a bad emotion or modeled abusive anger need a better perspective about anger for allowing them to feel and process it in healthy ways.

Aristotle commended a good kind of anger that is "neither too hasty nor too slow-tempered." He spoke of not being too easily provoked to anger and being free from bitterness and contentiousness, of maintaining "tranquility and stability of spirit".[3]

4. Spiritual Restoration: A lesson from AA

The organization *Alcoholics Anonymous* is well known for its 12-step program developed to help free people from the controlling power of alcohol addiction. The 12 steps have two prominent themes that are stated explicitly in the first two steps.

> **Step 1**: We admitted we were powerless over alcohol — that our lives had become unmanageable.
>
> **Step 2**: We came to believe that a power greater than ourselves could restore us to sanity.[4]

Most recovering alcoholics admit that these two steps are crucial to their ongoing freedom from the controlling power of alcohol. They also acknowledge that an alcoholic's unwillingness to admit that he is powerless is a clear warning sign of his return to alcohol.

What AA recognized about gaining freedom from the addictive power of alcohol is the same thing many people acknowledge about overcoming the effects of a troubled upbringing. We cannot do it on our strength; we need the power of God to restore us.

Choosing a greater power

Discounting the spiritual dimension of restoration is a mistake. Yet identifying the spiritual *solution* is not easy. There are many kinds of spirituality. Some brands are too vague to be a power greater than ourselves. Others are toxic and cause more harm than good.

I ask for your permission to share my understanding of this greater power. When it comes to different versions of spiritual knowledge, I have investigated this matter based on one central question: What version of the spiritual corresponds most with reality? Or, which version of spirituality is most plausible in light of what I see and know about humanity, the observable world, and its history?

After examining a vast array of options, I concluded that a Christian worldview offers the most logically consistent and plausibly realistic understanding of life and the world. It just simply offers the best explanation of the world I encounter each day. And it offers the best account covering the most extensive range of evidence in the world and in the human spirit.

The Christian worldview speaks in profoundly satisfying ways about shared human feelings and concerns. At its core, it provides a reason for the universal longing for meaningful and hopeful existence and everyday human needs for love, forgiveness, and peace. Unlike other options, it explains the twofold reality of dignity and depravity so clearly observed in human beings—amazing acts of human heroism and benevolence and horrible acts of evil. I cannot find any other spiritual understanding that corresponds with reality as comprehensively as Christianity.

The main story of the Christian Bible is God's pursuing love for his fallen creation—longing to forgive them and restore them to his image and likeness. Bishop Lesslie Newbigin summarized it well...

> If, in fact, it is true that Almighty God, creator and sustainer of all that exists in heaven and on earth, has—at a known time and place in human history—so humbled himself as to become part of our sinful humanity, and to suffer and die a shameful death to take away our sin, and to rise from the dead as the first-fruit of a new creation, if this is a fact, then to affirm it is not arrogance. To remain quiet about it is treason to our fellow human beings. If it is really true, as it is, that

"the Son of God loved me and gave himself up for me," how can I agree that this amazing act of matchless grace should merely become part of a syllabus for the "comparative study of religions"?[5]

The rest of the story

With this pivotal restorative dimension of life as our topic, let's return to some of the people you met earlier in the book for the rest of their story.

Hurt by a distant father (Julie's story, chapter seven)

After seeking spiritual and medical counsel, Julie began to receive the help she needed. It was as though God began to whisper to her soul...

> It was never about you, Julie. You could never be good enough to earn my love. You need to stop wasting so much energy chasing empty goals. I will complete you. I will be the loving Father you never had. Stop striving. Stop pretending. Stop expecting your husband to fulfill my role in your life. You are my daughter and I love you, especially when you have nothing to give. I made you and I like what I made. Enter into my love. Be healed, find rest and be whole. You are mine and you are deeply loved. Nothing will ever change my love.

She clings to these words during her dark days because the battle continues. She realizes that full healing might not ever be experienced in this life, but she finally has the hope that she will survive.

For the first time in her life, she began to hear the reality of the truth about her past. Identifying what she is up against gave her a stronger defense against it. She is learning each day to draw satisfaction from being known and loved by God. Although Julie is in a much better place in her life, she is still tempted to believe that she is not good enough to receive love from anyone and she is learning how to speak truth to her mind when she is assailed with doubt and disapproval.

"My great-grandfather affected four generations"
(John's story, chapter six)

> My dad and I agree that although Grandpa suffered greatly, his lifelong fight against self-pity, bitterness, and revenge contributed to a legacy for which I am grateful. In many ways, my grandfather is my hero for his desire and effort to honor God as best he could despite being rejected by his parents.

A quiet domineering father (Lisa's story, introduction to chapter four)

> I prayed, "Lord, help me to be able to turn around." I did not want to turn around. I had to come to realize that there was a sense of power that came with what I did. As long as I was like that, I was in the driver's seat, making my husband come after me and prove to me that he wanted me by pleading with me. There was a small perverse sense of pleasure in that, I think.
> But still I said, "Lord, help me to be able to turn around." And the minute I said that, I physically felt something lift off of me. It was seriously a physical sensation, like a weight coming off, or falling off, or

something. And I immediately turned around and looked him in the eye.

When that happened, it finally dawned on me that what was happening there was a thing in the spiritual realms. I might have thought I was in control by acting the way I was, but I wasn't. I was a prisoner to my past and I was reveling in it, thinking it was giving me power. There was no way I could have done that on my own. It was such a physical thing.

I remember thinking to myself, "I shouldn't be doing this. I really should talk to him," but I felt entirely unable to do it. The bonds of imprisonment were really strong. All it took was that very simple prayer, one small request for help, for me to feel the chains completely fall away. Knowing that seemed to break a lot of the appeal of acting that way for me, and it was after that that I began to slowly start to change how I responded to conflict. I still had to continually choose the light God offered and reject the habits from my past. But it became easier to choose God after that, and He's been completely faithful in giving me the power to change.

I came to understand how the survival mechanisms we learn to get through our childhood are used to hold us captive and keep us from getting better. We have to see it that way and choose to ask God into the situation in order to get better.

Another person who was instrumental in helping me change was a close friend. She overcame a past full of horrible abuses. She is a person who is gifted with a strong discerning spirit and a unique blend of compassion and a no-nonsense approach to life. I needed someone like this in my life to confront me and to help me see things differently.

I remember my friend sharing the story of the lame man by the water in Bethesda [from John 5:2-6]. Christ didn't just make him well, he first asked, "Do you want to be well?"[6] A lot of times people don't want to be well. We have to pick up our mat and let the change happen, but sometimes we like sitting in our misery.

None of my change would have been possible apart from God. This is all the more apparent when I look at the rest of my family, who are all still wallowing in the effects of these things. God helped me see where I was wrong and gave me the courage to choose to change. It was always my choice, though—I could have said no to change and wallowed in my ways. But God presents my flaws to me and gives me the opportunity for something better. It is also because of Him that I know how to love. There was no expressed love in my home—no words, or hugs, or affirmations—and my sister doesn't know how to do those things.

Without God's love through Jesus Christ, I would be hardened, self-protective, critical and difficult to please (I know, because I see these tendencies in me)—in short—I'd be just like my dad.

God gave me the opportunity to change. Would I choose to live in fear or live in the security of His love for me? Would I let that fear turn to hatred and unforgiveness, or allow God to show me the love He has even for my father? This is a choice I find I am constantly having to renew. I forgive and love my father, but every once-in-a-while, the fear and anger come rearing back. But I have to choose to hold on to

God and His perspective, or I will drown in my own misery and take my family with me.

My father always used to say, "You can't control what anyone else does. But you can control how you react to them." Ironically, he used to be full of good advice like that which he seemed incapable of implementing himself. But it's always stayed with me. And it's true. I can't control what happened to me, or what still happens. But I can control my reaction to it. I can choose to look to God, who transforms me with his love and by renewing my mind. I can choose change.

Three essentials of the spiritual dimension

The spiritual dimension makes vital connections with other areas of life. Spirituality is not (to use an old expression) "pie in the sky by and by." Like the other three dimensions, it's a "here and now" reality. In fact, I would argue that it's not only necessary but foundational to restoring the whole person. Tipping the hat to spirituality as if it's a nice thing to add if it helps you is a disservice to those in need of rebuilding their lives. The spiritual dimension provides essential perspectives for shaping our thinking, emotions, and relationships. Three components that play a role in restoring the whole person are Scripture, prayer, and music.

Scripture

When I use the word Scripture, I mean the Christian Bible, a book written in a historical context but revealing truths that extend beyond time into eternity. Scripture makes a unique contribution in ways that relate to perspective formation.

Scripture connects the horizontal mess of life with the vertical. It invites me out of the swamp of a self-centered life to see God, my Maker and Redeemer, as the only worthy center of life. Scripture is not a book of positive thinking quotes from great life coaches, but one that provides a basis for belief in human dignity without flattering me with nonsense about how great I am. Whatever bad things others say about me, Scripture injects an unexpected liberating reality telling me that it's far worse than they understand. Whether my father called me a "dummy" or a "failure," Scripture has the power to set me free from the opinions of people in a strange way. First, it leads me to declare, "Oh, what a miserable person I am!" It then leads me to the solution for my miserableness: "Thank God! The answer is in Jesus Christ our Lord." (Romans 7:24-25, NLT)

Prayer

Prayer also provides a perspective-forming session with God. I concur with the author, Philip Yancey, when he writes,

> I pray to restore the truth of the universe, to gain a glimpse of the world, and me, through the eyes of God. In prayer, I shift my point of view away from my selfishness…
>
> Prayer is the act of seeing reality from God's point of view. Prayer has become for me much more than a shopping list of requests to present to God. It has become a realignment of everything.[7]

The serenity prayer also offers a helpful perspective: "God grant me the serenity to accept the things I cannot change, courage to change the things I can, and wisdom to know the difference."

I agree with my doctor that it is ignorantly inadequate to offer someone a "five-bible-verses-and-you'll-be-better" solution for depression. I also believe that Scripture and prayer play an essential role in helping people overcome a troubled upbringing and many of the struggles of this life. Unfortunately, we can easily lose perspective or only see our issues through the limited lens of one or two dimensions of human existence. We need holistic solutions that respect all dimensions of life.

Music

The human species appears universally designed for song and dance. Music is powerful. Research continues to demonstrate in fascinating ways the power of music in therapy and recovery.[8] Music conveys a message in ways that enhance our attention, connect deeply with our emotions, and remain in our memory. A meaningful song that integrates the spiritual with the challenge of overcoming a painful past is appropriately titled, "Redeemed."

> Seems like all I can see was the struggle,
> Haunted by ghosts that lived in my past.
> Bound up in shackles of all my failures,
> Wondering how long is this gonna last.
> Then You look at this prisoner and say to me, "Son,
> Stop fighting a fight that's already been won."
> I am redeemed, You set me free!
> So I'll shake off these heavy chains
> And wipe away every stain...
> Now I'm not who I used to be.
> I am redeemed. I'm redeemed.

All my life I have been called unworthy,
Named by the voice of my shame and regret.
But when I hear You whisper,
"Child lift up your head,"
I remember oh God, You're not done with me yet.
I am redeemed, You set me free!
So I'll shake off these heavy chains
And wipe away every stain...
Now I'm not who I used to be.
Because I don't have to be the old man inside of me.
'Cause his day is long dead and gone.
Because I've got a new name, a new life,
I'm not the same, and a hope that will carry me home.
I am redeemed, You set me free!
So I'll shake off these heavy chains
And wipe away every stain now I'm not who I used to
be. Oh God I'm not who I used to be...
Jesus I'm not who I used to be
'Cause I am redeemed. Thank God, redeemed.[9]

One more story...

Wake Up! You're an Adult Now!
(Francine's story—holding onto the hope of restoring the
whole person)

Did you ever feel like your life started without you?
One day you awoke, and here you are in your 30's,
married, a career, kids, and wondering where you were
when this all took place? This is me!
I'll never forget the day I awoke in a counselor's office,
[with the counselor] telling me I was suffering from

PTSD. No, that wasn't me, nothing so wrong happened to me. She must be talking about someone else. The pieces did not seem to fit. I was a wife, married for ten years, a mom of a 2-year-old, and an RN who decided to be a stay-at-home mom for the past two years. I was who I was, but something was knocking at the door. That something was my life knocking, saying, "You cannot sleep anymore. Wake up; you're an adult now."

Months before being diagnosed with PTSD, I went to see many doctors, had many tests, and no one could figure out the source of my symptoms. Medically I was clear, healthy; mentally I was crumbling. I had not slept in three months; I was having dizzy spells, nightmares and suicidal thoughts. My husband eventually stayed home with me as I became nonfunctioning. I could not even care for my son. I was afraid—lost all hope. I wanted answers and fast. I agreed to speak with a counselor after taking numerous sleeping pills, anti-anxiety meds, and antidepressants—which just made everything worse.

I thought the counselor would figure out what medicine I needed, and everything would be back to "normal." Little did I know my "normal" was not me at all, but a whole other life I didn't even know existed. I always knew growing up of an instance with my uncle who had molested me. It was reported to the school, but nothing ever came of it. So, I thought I would just move on. It only happened once, right?!

My counseling sessions became a weekly part of my life. I was determined to get better and fast. Then a bomb went off, and I fell deeper and deeper into depression, fear and worry. In sessions, I started having memories, "flashbacks" of horrible things. It was like I was watching a movie and I was the star; however, I was also in the front row waiting for it for the first time.

The reality was I had been severely traumatized from a very young age. Most of my perpetrators were people who you are supposed to be able to love and trust. My uncle, stepdad, stepbrother, and family friends repeatedly sexually abused me. Even my mother would hand me over to these men—a harsh reality even now as I write about it. Eventually, I also saw myself handing myself over to these men.

After many painful memories, it was clear I was trained very well to do as these men wanted me to do. When I would see myself fight back, they would beat me down verbally, on occasion physically, and there was always fear driven in that they would kill me or even worse. I was repeatedly told to hurt or kill myself if I ever said anything. For me, this was normal. My whole life had revolved around these horrible things; darkness, secrecy, keeping it hidden. That was one me; then there was the other me.

The other me went to school and got good grades. I had trouble making and keeping friends. We moved around a lot. I did graduate from high school. I was determined to get out of the house and be on my own. I became an LPN, met my husband, was married, started working full time, and enrolled in an RN program. I thought I had escaped, but no, it was just the other me covering up for the one me.

The men would call, I would be ready and go to wherever they told me. I always had a cover story for my other life, and of course, the two me's could no longer ignore each other. I had pretty much disconnected from my original self, blacked out the horrible things, and the disconnect carried over into my other life as well.

My relationship with my husband and my kids suffered the most. I was emotionally and mentally unavailable to them. I had to learn how to stay grounded in my present life. I learned to do this step by step, with counseling, prayer and growing my trust and relationship with God. Now I can function more as an adult, not respond as a child. My marriage is stronger today. I am beginning to bond with my children much better. I am still holding on to the hope of restoring the whole person.

Chapter 13: Evaluation and Discussion

1. Have you applied the four dimensions of life and the three primary expressions of personhood to your plan for life? (Explain)

2. Summarize what you found helpful regarding physical restoration.

3. Summarize what you found helpful under social restoration.

4. Can you identify in any way with the self-doubt and insecurity described under social restoration? (Explain)

5. How does insecurity sabotage relationships?

6. How does a self-limiting belief system affect relationships?

7. Do you recognize evidences of a self-limiting belief system in your life? (Explain)

8. Summarize what you found helpful regarding psychological restoration.

9. What did you find helpful regarding the role of the spiritual dimension in restoration?

Appendix I: An 18-Year Factor Inventory

Stop, listen and learn from the past.

Failure to take your 18-year factor seriously is not good for you or for those who are close to you. Sometimes it's not a matter of "just getting over it" or putting it behind you! Let the process begin by courageously and honestly assessing your childhood experiences.

Finish the following sentences:

1. When I think about my childhood years...(Include reference to significant disruptions or serious dysfunctions if applicable)

2. When I think back on the way my parents related to me... (Include the parenting style used to raise you)

3. I can see how my upbringing affects my thoughts, feelings, beliefs, actions, and relationships in the following ways...
   - Thoughts
   - Feelings
   - Beliefs
   - Relationships (Use Appendix II to help evaluate this)

4. During my childhood years, I turned to the following protective mechanisms...

5. Due to an experience during my childhood years, I allowed the following emotional drug(s) to control my heart… (Describe the ongoing effects)

- Resentment
- Anger
- Hatred
- Bitterness
- Self-pity
- Self-loathing
- Shame
- Guilt
- Fear

6. Out of the four kinds of children described in chapter nine, I identify most with… (Explain why)

1. The Angry Rebel ("Our black sheep")
2. The Peacemaking Mediator ("Our good child")
3. The Depressed Defeatist ("Our emotional child")
4. The Fleeing Perfectionist ("Our trophy")

7. The experience of writing my story affected me in the following ways…

The Adverse Childhood Experiences (ACE) Study uses ten questions to assess childhood trauma.[1] If the answer is "yes," check the box preceding the question(s).

Prior to your 18th birthday:

1. ☐ Did a parent or other adult in the household often or very often... Swear at you, insult you, put you down, or humiliate you? or Act in a way that made you afraid that you might be physically hurt?

2. ☐ Did a parent or other adult in the household often or very often... Push, grab, slap, or throw something at you? or Ever hit you so hard that you had marks or were injured?

3. ☐ Did an adult or person at least 5 years older than you ever... Touch or fondle you or have you touch their body in a sexual way? or Attempt or actually have oral, anal, or vaginal intercourse with you?

4. ☐ Did you often or very often feel that ... No one in your family loved you or thought you were important or special? or Your family didn't look out for each other, feel close to each other, or support each other?

5. ☐ Did you often or very often feel that ... You didn't have enough to eat, had to wear dirty clothes, and had no one to protect you? or Your parents were too drunk or high to take care of you or take you to the doctor if you needed it?

6. ☐ Was a biological parent ever lost to you through divorce, abandonment, or other reason ?

7. ☐ Was your mother or stepmother: Often or very often pushed, grabbed, slapped, or had something

thrown at her? or Sometimes, often, or very often
kicked, bitten, hit with a fist, or hit with something
hard? or Ever repeatedly hit over at least a few minutes
or threatened with a gun or knife?

8. ☐ Did you live with anyone who was a problem
drinker or alcoholic, or who used street drugs?

9. ☐ Was a household member depressed or mentally ill,
or did a household member attempt suicide?

10. ☐ Did a household member go to prison?

Appendix II: Evaluating the effects of your 18-year factor on current relationships

Circle or highlight the ones that honestly describe you and explain why. Consider allowing someone close to you to assess your answers.

1. Do you need to be in control in relationships?

2. Do you try to manipulate others?

3. Do you block accessibility to your emotions?

4. Do you second-guess the motives of others?

5. Do you doubt the sincerity of others?

6. Do you fear commitment?

7. Do you crave attention?

8. Do you fear rejection from others?

9. Do you need continual reaffirmation?

10. Do you isolate yourself from others?

11. Do you feel unsafe in relationships?

12. Do you tend to push people away?

13. Do you feel disconnected from others?

14. Do you struggle with trusting others?

15. Do you fear loss of a relationship?

16. Do you become quickly irritated with others?

17. Do you read into words and actions of others?

18. Do relationships make you feel stressed out?

19. Do you put up walls to keep others out?

20. Do you avoid talking about personal matters?

21. Do you tend to shut down or use silent treatment with others?

22. Do you find it difficult to admit you're wrong?

23. Do you tend to be argumentative in relationships?

24. Do fear, control or guilt-play a role in your relationships?

25. Do you need the affirmations of others to feel good about yourself?

26. Do you treat strangers better than those who are close to you?

NOTES

Introduction

1. https://georgetownta.wordpress.com/2015/03/05/who-needs-to-pay-attention-to-the-acc-study.
2. https://www.wired.com/2016/06/steven-spielberg-the-bfg.
3. http://time.com/4351287/steven-spielberg-grad-speech.

Chapter 5

1. Hustad, Megan. "Surprising Benefits for Those Who Had Tough Childhoods." https://www.psychologytoday.com/us/articles/201703/surprising-benefits-those-who-had-tough-childhoods?amp.

Chapter 6

1. Wallerstein, et al. Introduction, p xxix-xxxii.
2. United States Department of Health and Human Services, Administration for Children and Families, Administration on Children, Youth and Families, Children's Bureau. Child Maltreatment Survey, 2012 (2013).
3. U.S. Bureau of Justice Statistics. Sexual Assault of Young Children as Reported to Law Enforcement. 2000.

Chapter 7

1. Horowitz, A.V., & Wakefield, J.C. p. 4.
2. Ibid.

3. Streep, Peg. "The Enduring Pain of Childhood Verbal Abuse." https://www.psychologytoday.com/us/blog/tech-support/201611/the-enduring-pain-childhood-verbal-abuse.

Chapter 9

1. "Early Life Stress and Depression." https://www.mdedge.com/psychiatry/article/61018/early-life-stress-and-depression-childhood-trauma-may-lead.
2. Hustad, Megan. "Surprising Benefits for Those Who Had Tough Childhoods." https://www.psychologytoday.com/us/articles/201703/surprising-benefits-those-who-had-tough-childhoods.

Chapter 11

1. "Drug and Alcohol Detox and the Symptoms of Withdrawal." https://recoverycentersofamerica.com/treatment/detox/.
2. https://haitiancreole.net/behind-mountains-haitian-proverb/.
3. https://vault.sierraclub.org/john_muir_exhibit/life/life_and_letters/chapter_10.aspx.
4. Plantinga, p. 132-133.

Chapter 12

1. https://www.nbcnews.com/pop-culture/movies/claude-lanzmann-director-holocaust-documentary-shoah-dies-age-92-n888971.
2. Thomas, Gary. "The Forgiveness Factor." https://www.christianitytoday.com/ct/2000/january10/1.38.html.
3. https://www.cdc.gov/violenceprevention/childabuseandneglect/acestudy/about.html.

Chapter 13

1. https://www.acesconnection.com/g/foster-children-parents-support-network/blog/7-ways-childhood-adversity-can-actually-change-your-brain-goodmenproject-com.
2. https://developingchild.harvard.edu/resources/inbrief-the-impact-of-early-adversity-on-childrens-development/.
3. http://classics.mit.edu/Aristotle/nicomachaen.4.iv.html.
4. https://www.aa.org/assets/en_US/smf-121_en.pdf.
5. Newbigin, Lesslie. "Comments on the 50th Anniversary of Tambaram, 1988." http://newbiginhouse.org/wp-content/uploads/2015/08/Missionary-to-India_Sherman.pdf.
6. John 5:2-6. Bible, New International Version. https://www.biblegateway.com/passage/?search=John+5%3A2-6&version=NIV.
7. Yancey, p. 29.

8. Merz, Beverly. "Healing Through Music." https://www.health.harvard.edu/blog/healing-through-music-201511058556.

9. Cowart, Benji, Weaver, Michael, & Weaver, Michael David (2012). "Redeemed." Warner/Chappell Music, Inc. Recorded by Big Daddy Weave.

Appendix I

1. http://acestoohigh.com/aces-101/.

BIBLIOGRAPHY
for further study

Blazer, D. G. (2005). *The Age of Melancholy: "Major Depression" and Its Social Origins.* New York: Routledge.

Cherlin, A. J. (2009). *The Marriage-Go-Round: The State of Marriage and the Family in America Today.* New York: Alfred A. Knopf.

Hallowell, E. M., & Ratey, J. J. (1995). *Driven to Distraction: Recognizing and Coping with Attention Deficit Disorder From Childhood Through Adulthood.* New York: Simon & Schuster.

Healy, D. (2003). *The Antidepressant Era.* Cambridge, MA: Harvard University Press.

Helming, D. M. (1997). *The Examined Life: The Art of Knowing, Owning, and Giving Yourself.* Dallas, TX: Spence Publishing Company.

Horowitz, A. V., & Wakefield, J. C. (2007). *The Loss of Sadness: How Psychiatry Transformed Normal Sorrow Into Depressive Disorder.* New York: Oxford University Press.

Plantinga, Cornelius (1996). *Not the Way It's Supposed to Be: A Breviary of Sin.* Grand Rapids, MI: Wm. B. Eerdmans Publishing Co.

Smith, C. (2003). *Moral, Believing Animals: Human Personhood and Culture.* Oxford: Oxford University Press.

Waite, L. J., & Gallagher, M. (2000). *The Case for Marriage: Why Married People are Happier, Healthier, and Better Off Financially.* New York: Broadway Books.

Wallerstein, J. S., Lewis, J., & Blakeslee, S. (2000). *The Unexpected Legacy of Divorce: A 25 Year Landmark Study.* New York: Hyperion.

Whiteman, T., Novotni, M., & Petersen, R. (1995). *Adult ADD: A Reader Friendly Guide to Identifying, Understanding, and Treating Adult Attention Deficit Disorder.* Colorado Springs, CO: Piñon Press.

Yancey, Philip D. (2006). Prayer: Does It Make Any Difference? Grand Rapids, MI: Zondervan.

Words of appreciation

It is hard to list all the people to whom I am grateful for the completion of this book. My wife, Becky Cornell, allowed me (without complaint) many extra hours for writing. My staff encouraged me in many ways to finish *The 18-Year Factor*. My editor, Laura Xentaras, worked tirelessly and faithfully. Sandy Cove Conference Center on the Chesapeake Bay in North East, Maryland graciously provided me with an exquisite place for writing.

CPSIA information can be obtained
at www.ICGtesting.com
Printed in the USA
BVHW082155010120
568341BV00001B/121/P